A NARRATIVE APPROACH TO ORGANIZATION STUDIES

BARBARA CZARNIAWSKA
Gothenburg University

Qualitative Research Methods
Volume 43

Sage Publications
International Educational and Professional Publisher
Thousand Oaks   London   New Delhi

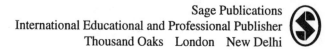

For information:

 SAGE Publications, Inc.
2455 Teller Road
Thousand Oaks, California 91320
e-mail: order@sagepub.com

SAGE Publications Ltd.
6 Bonhill Street
London EC2A 4PU
United Kingdom

SAGE Publications India Pvt. Ltd.
M-32 Market
Greater Kailash I
New Delhi 110 048 India

Printed in the United States of America

Library of Congress Cataloging-in-Publication Data

Czarniawska-Joerges, Barbara.
    A narrative approach to organization studies / by Barbara
Czarniawska.
        p.   cm. — (Qualitative research methods ; v. 43)
        Includes bibliographical references.
        ISBN 0-7619-0662-2 (acid-free paper). — ISBN 0-7619-0663-0 (pbk.:
acid-free paper)
        1. Social sciences—Research—Methodology. 2. Social sciences—
Methodology. I. Title. II. Series.
    H62.C93 1998
    300'.72—dc21   97-21225

This book is printed on acid-free paper.

98 99 00 01 02 03 10 9 8 7 6 5 4 3 2 1

Acquisitions Editor:	Peter Labella
Editorial Assistant:	Corinne Pierce
Production Editor:	Sanford Robinson
Production Assistant:	Karen Wiley
Typesetter:	Rebecca Evans
Print Buyer:	Anna Chin

CONTENTS

SERIES EDITORS' INTRODUCTION

Narrative, stories, and tales, it is said, connect the person and the personal to social events, processes, and organizations. Most work in narratives concerns "personal narratives" or stories, some of which bridge the person and the social, yet little work as been done that connects roles and organizations. Qualitative research using narrative methods enables researchers to place themselves at the interface between persons, stories, and organizations, and to place the person in emotional and organizational context.

Barbara Czarniawska has long cultivated the narrative tradition and argued for the links between roles and organization as a part of organizational analysis. She sees organization, indeed like a story, as a social construction that is interactionally relevant and constraining. Her book is a clear guide to conceptualizing organization, connecting it to sentiments and action, and revealing it through stories. In this sense, she shares the concerns of Feldman (Volume 33), Schwartzman (Volume 27), and Reissman (Volume 30), in applying narrative methods to qualitative research.

John Van Maanen
Peter K. Manning
Marc L. Miller

PREFACE

This monograph presents a specific approach to organization studies in the field while simultaneously illustrating its use. The book is mainly directed toward graduate students in business and public administration, sociology, anthropology, and political sciences, that is, all social sciences that practice fieldwork in contemporary societies. It emerged as a result of teaching graduate courses in Scandinavia and throughout the world. This experience taught me that graduate students often have problems not in choosing a method but in describing it in an acceptable manner. One could argue that the problem is circular: Students cannot describe the method because they do not know why they chose it in the first place. They follow a logic of appropriateness, as March and Olsen (1989) call the reasoning that forms an action imperative based on the observation that "everyone is doing qualitative methods right now." Dissertations, however, call for a logic of justification and here, deprived of positivist props, students feel lost. They are unable to conduct a methodological reasoning of their own: What do I want to know? How am I going to learn that? What are the alternatives? They often borrow pieces of other people's reasoning (which is the only way to do it) but fail to patch them together into a convincing whole. This monograph is intended to help them do so, by way of reflection and example.

The book is based on the assumption that there is no method, strictly speaking, in social sciences. All there is are other works as sources of inspiration, an array of various techniques, and a systematic reflection on the work that is being done. The approach presented is inspired by the works of Mikhail Bakhtin, Jerome Bruner, Umberto Eco, Karin Knorr Cetina, Bruno Latour, Deirdre McCloskey, Richard Rorty, and David Silverman. Thus, it joins various disciplines (from literary theory through psychology, sociology of knowledge, and economics to philosophy) and various geographic areas of influence (with a "natural" European bias).

This monograph assumes that research consists of collecting and producing texts as well as accounting for a certain social practice (in this case, *organizing*). Researchers collect and interpret texts produced in the field where the practice takes place, but in the process they create such texts themselves: interview records, field notes, observation records, diaries, and the report itself. Although a large part of research, like any other professional practice, consists of conversations—with other people and other texts—it is the inscription that finalizes research.

The specificity of the approach presented here is that the nucleus is attributed to one type of the text—the narrative—although the importance of other types, such as lists, tables, taxonomies, and number sheets, is not denied. It is nevertheless narratives—that is, texts that present events developing in time according to (impersonal) causes or (human) intentions—that are the main carriers of knowledge in modern societies toward the end of the 20th century.

The examples are taken from ethnographically oriented organization studies from Melville Dalton through John Van Maanen to Gideon Kunda. As far as my own work is concerned, I draw on experience gathered during 25 years of field organization studies in Poland, the United States, Italy, and Sweden, with special focus on methodological reflection as developed in *Narrating the Organization* (1997a). The present text benefited from incisive comments from Bernward Joerges, to whom I owe special thanks, and the editorial comments of John Van Maanen, to whom I owe continuous thanks. Joan Acker commented on Chapter 3, and Richard Rottenburg helped me locate certain esoteric references in anthropology, for which I am truly grateful. I thank Nancy Adler and Ann McKinnon for correcting my English.

Zeichnung zum Unstern der Schiffe (Paul Klee, 1917)

1 CONCOCTING A DEVICE
The Narrative in Social Sciences and Organization Studies

William James (1890/1950) postulated that the world is accessible as a buzzing, pulsating, formless mass of signals, out of which people try to make sense, into which they attempt to introduce order, and from which they construct figures against a background that remains undifferentiated. They do it to be able to act on the world and therefore do it continuously and for the most part unreflectively. Being technologically minded, people are also able to construct instruments to facilitate such endeavors intentionally; they call these *methods, theories, paradigms,* and *frames.* Each label is embedded in its own way, and to choose one is to choose the context into which it leads. Here, I opt for the term coined by the Russian formalists (Bakhtin/Medvedev, 1928/1985), that is, *device,* with which one tackles a *material* at hand. A device is at the same time more vague and more specific than a method. It promises artfulness and instrumentality, but not necessarily high tech and standardization. Unlike a method, a device can be idiosyncratic; therefore I am speaking of *concocting* one.

I intend to show how to concoct a device for shaping organization studies out of such ingredients as literary theory, anthropology, and sociology (in particular, the new institutionalist school) in the hope of selling not so much the product as the process. Readers are encouraged to concoct their own devices.

On Narrative

The central ingredient of my device is the notion of narrative, and this is where I begin:

> An engineer joined a foreign company seven years ago. During that time, she became a top figure in the R&D department at the company headquarters, having produced several innovations and published several articles in journals in her specialty. At the recent job appraisal session, however, the customary tenure and promotion that comes after seven years with the company was refused her. (Czarniawska & Calàs, in press)

A narrative, in its most basic form, requires at least three elements: an original state of affairs, an action or an event, and the consequent state of affairs. I am using a narrow definition of narrative here (see Greimas & Courtés, 1982, p. 203), unlike, for example, Barthes (1966/1977, p. 79), who includes any form of communication in his notion of narrative. These three elements could also be presented as a list:

1. An engineer joins a foreign company.
2. An engineer acquires an international reputation.
3. An engineer is refused promotion.

Listed in this way, the events do not make much sense. For them to become a narrative, they require a *plot,* that is, some way to bring them into a meaningful whole. The easiest way to do this is by introducing chronology (and then . . .), which in the mind of the reader easily turns into causality (as a result of, in spite of). Observe that if the two last elements on the list are put in a reverse chronological order (the engineer was refused promotion and then acquired a professional reputation), the story changes completely. Also observe that the plot must be *put* there, which is seen as a problem in scientific texts: "the plot of a historical narrative is always an embarrassment and has to be presented as 'found' in the events rather than put there by narrative techniques" (White, 1973, p. 20). In anthropology, this became acutely obvious when the dominant plot of the discipline changed dramatically: from acculturation ("the present as disorganization, the past as glorious, and the future as assimilation") to liberation ("the present . . . as a resistance movement, the past as exploitation, and the future as ethnic resurgence"; E. M. Bruner, 1986, p. 139). The plot built around the passage from a nostalgic past to a modern future changed into a plot built around the passage from an imperialist exploitation to an reenactment of the past, and it keeps changing (see Sahlins, 1994).

A story may contain an explicitly formulated point (all so-called educational narratives do), or else readers are supposed to provide one: "She was discriminated against, like many women before her" or "The company demanded more of its employees." As can be seen in this simple example, basic narratives can carry a load of ambiguity and therefore leave openings for negotiation of meaning: "She was simply not good enough. She could not possibly have been discriminated against! At the turn of the 21st century?" "You must be joking. Just look at what her male colleagues did to deserve promotion."

By the criteria of scientific (paradigmatic) knowledge, the knowledge carried by narratives is not very impressive. Formal logic rarely guides the reasoning, the level of abstraction is low, and the causal links may be established in a wholly arbitrary way. As French philosopher Lyotard (1979/1986) points out, the legitimacy of scientific knowledge in its modern and western meaning depends on its sharp differentiation from the commonsense, everyday knowledge of ordinary people—the narrative knowledge that tells of human projects and their consequences as they unfold over time. Yet it has been claimed that the narrative is the main mode of human knowledge (J. Bruner, 1986, 1990) and the main mode of communication (Fisher, 1984, 1987).

Reconciliation between scientific and narrative knowledge has been attempted now and again. In modern times, the examples of such attempts start with the work of Giambattista Vico (1744/1960) and continue with the realist novel (see Lepenies, 1988; Czarniawska-Joerges & Guillet de Monthoux, 1994) and the Chicago School of Sociology (e.g., Cappetti, 1995). How can these attempts be justified?

Alasdaire MacIntyre (1981/1990), a moral philosopher, claims that social life is best conceived of as an enacted narrative. This is a thought resonant with that of philosopher, poet, and literary theorist Kenneth Burke (1945/1969), who suggests a *dramatist* analysis of human conduct, which he bases on the assumption that the rules of the drama as much reflect as influence and shape social life.

In principle, there are many possible ways of conceiving of human action. In many organization theory texts, the term *action* is replaced by, or used as, a synonym of behavior. *Organizational behavior* is a term that is taken for granted, unproblematic even for otherwise critical authors and readers. But the difference between action and behavior is crucial for social theory. The notion of "behavioral sciences" goes back to 18th-century empiricism, in which the "sense datum" was proposed as the main unit of cognition and the main object of scientific study. If we were to describe our experience in terms of sensory descriptions, however, "we would be confronted not only with uninterpreted, but an uninterpretable world" (MacIntyre, 1981/1990, p. 79). Such a world would indeed be a world of behavior, both meaningless and mechanical, because if sense data were to become the basis for the formulation of laws, all reference to intentions, purposes, and reasons—all that changes human behavior into human action—would have to be removed.

It is impossible to understand human conduct by ignoring its intentions, and it is impossible to understand human intentions by ignoring the settings in which they make sense (Schütz, 1973b). Such settings may be institutions, sets of practices, or some other contexts created by humans and nonhumans—contexts that have a history, that have been organized as narratives themselves. Particular deeds and whole histories of individual actors have to be situated to be intelligible. "The engineer has been refused promotion" is a meaningless sentence; if it is to acquire meaning, it must be situated in the life history of this engineer or in the history of the profession or the company.

The advantages of building a connection between the theory of human action and the narrative has also been pointed out by Ricoeur (1981), who suggests that meaningful action is to be considered as a text and text as an action. Meaningful action shares the constitutive features of the text: It becomes objectified by inscription, which frees it from its agents. It has relevance beyond its immediate context and it can be read like an "open text." The theory of interpretation can thus be extended to the field of social sciences.

But will social science lose more than it will gain if such extension is to take place? Polkinghorne (1987), following Ricoeur's (1981) reasoning, points out that a special type of explanation is possible only in a narrative. Only there can "understanding" be reconciled with "explanation" in an interpretation of the text. Hermeneutics and semiotics, two sets of devices, can be combined in the same way that motives are reconciled with causes in an interpretation of human action and justification is interwoven with causality in human beliefs (Rorty, 1991). This combination is looked down on within science but is taken as obvious in the narrative: "Tough competition made companies sharpen their personnel policy rules, which had often been used as a pretext to discriminate against female employees."

Within "the logo-scientific mode of knowing," as Bruner (1990) calls it, an explanation is achieved by recognizing an event as an instant of general law or as belonging to a certain category: "Female engineers above 40 are promoted less often than their male peers." Within "the narrative mode of knowing," an explanation consists in relating an event to human projects: "Her talents and commitment were neglected by the chauvinist management." Sensemaking (see Weick, 1995) consists of attempts to integrate a new event into a plot, by which it becomes understandable in relation to the context of what has happened. "Thus, narratives *exhibit* an explanation instead of demonstrating it" (Polkinghorne, 1987, p. 21).

Although it is clear that the narrative offers an alternative mode of knowing, the relative advantage of using this mode may remain uncertain. Bruner (1990) points out that the strength of the narrative lies in its indifference to extralinguistic reality (p. 44). In narrative, the perceived coherence of the sequence (temporal order) of events rather than the truth or falsity of story elements determines the plot and thus the power of the narrative as a story. A story that says "The engineer was refused promotion, and then she went skiing," that is, a story with an incomprehensible plot, will need some additional elements to make sense, even though the two events and their temporal connection may be true and correct in themselves. In other words, there are no structural differences between fictional and factual narratives, and their respective attraction is not determined by their claim to be fact or fiction. Paul Veyne (1988), a French historian, studied the notion of truth in history and said that

> a world cannot be inherently fictional; it can be fictional only according to whether one believes in it or not. The difference between fiction and reality is not objective and does not pertain to the thing itself: it resides in us, according to whether or not we subjectively see in it a fiction. (p. 21)

The interpretation of a narrative—both of its status (fact or fiction?) and of its point (discrimination or not?)—is situationally negotiated or, rather, arrived at, because contingency plays as much a part in the process as aesthetics or politics. Although the narrative may be indifferent to extralinguistic reality, it compensates for it with an extreme sensibility to the linguistic reality.

These characteristics of the narrative are noted by most of the analysts of the narrative but are then often put aside with some embarrassment, to be triumphantly dragged out again by the advocates of the logico-scientific mode of knowing. What kind of knowledge is it that does not allow for recognizing whether or not a story is true or invented?

Bruner (1990) claims that this peculiarity of narrative accounts for most of its power. People's nonscientific explanations and interpretations of life events are grounded in attempts to establish a connection between the exceptional and the ordinary. The ordinary, that which is "normal," "usual," and expected, acquires legitimacy and authority. The narrative, however, also has effective means at its disposal for rendering the unexpected intelligible. "The function of the narrative is to find an intentional state that mitigates, or at least makes comprehensible, a deviation from a canonical cultural pattern" (Bruner, 1990, pp. 49-50).

Because stories explaining deviations are socially sensitive, a story whose power does not reside in the difference between fact and fiction is convenient for such negotiations. Several of many alternative readings are always in the offing, as the examples quoted above show. The events acquire a meaning by the application of abduction, which introduces a hypothetical connection. Yet another reading ("The company changed its promotion rules, and as a result . . . ") might offer a better or more convincing explanation without challenging the truth or falsity of the story elements. We now have several readings of the story about the engineer and the lack of promotion built around the same event. There is no way of deciding among them except by negotiation—between the author and the reader (by which the author tries to get the upper hand but the reader gets the last word), or, as in organizational life, between various readers as actors. Stories, Bruner (1990) notes, are especially viable instruments for social negotiation.

This is all very well as long as it concerns everyday narratives. But can stories acquire a legitimate place in science? After some resistance, the insights on which scientific knowledge is grounded in metaphorical thinking have been more or less commonly accepted (thanks to writers such as Kuhn, 1962; McCloskey, 1986; and Morgan, 1986). Stories have a harder time. Yet, economics, McCloskey (1990) says, is full of stories and metaphors and this is how it should be: Metaphors condense stories and stories examine metaphors. Patriarchy is one metaphor that could be illustrated by the story above; but there are perhaps better stories for this metaphor and better metaphors for this story. "Stories criticize metaphors and metaphors criticize stories" (McCloskey, 1990, p. 96).

Stories and metaphors cannot replace one another because they have different tasks to accomplish. A narrative is a mode of association, of putting different things together (and, and, and), whereas metaphor is a mode of substitution (or, or, or; Latour, 1988). Alternatives to a narrative are lists and formal logic. An alternative to a metaphoric mode of substitution is, for instance, labeling, that is, giving proper names to objects and phenomena. There is a convention, however, that apportions different modes of association and substitution to different fields (science, literature) and different times (premodern, modern).

Narrative, Literature, and Science

The traditional view is that science should keep to facts and logic, leaving metaphors and stories to literature, this being a sediment of premodern times and oral societies. McCloskey (1990) points out that, contrary to this received wisdom, the sciences can be said to be using a tetrad of rhetorical figures: stories, metaphors, facts (which I call *lists,* to denote the enumeration of free-standing indexed statements such as names or dates, with no links between them), and formal logic. *Belles lettres* or folk theories mainly use stories and metaphors, although lists—of virtues, for example, or things required for a magical incantation—can also appear, although it is rare for them to use formal logic.

Rare but not nonexistent. Experimental writers and artists, such as Borges, Cortazar, Escher, and others with an inclination for linguistic and visual paradoxes, play with formal logic. On the other hand, social scientists seldom use formal logic—in the sense of the particular mode of reasoning, because all use logic in the sense of syntactic rules. What I want to emphasize is that science is not separated from literature by an abyss; over and above the publishers' classification, a work is attributed to a certain genre according to the frequency with which it uses certain rhetorical devices. Umberto Eco, who is a legitimate citizen in both worlds, put it as follows:

> I understand that, according to a current opinion, I have written some texts that can be labeled as scientific (or academic or theoretical), and some others which can be defined as creative. But I do not believe in such a straightforward distinction. I believe that Aristotle was as creative as Sophocles, and Kant as creative as Goethe. There is not some mysterious ontological difference between these two ways of writing. . . . The differences stand, first of all, in the propositional attitude of the writer, even though their propositional [attitude] is usually made evident by textual devices . . . (1992, p. 140)

We recognize a scientific text not because of its intrinsic scientific qualities but because the author claims it is scientific (and this claim can be contested) and because he or she uses textual devices that are conventionally considered scientific (and this convention is contested all the time). The genres blur in space (Geertz, 1980); do they also blur in time?

Comparative studies of literate and nonliterate societies (Goody, 1977, 1986) show that although narratives exist in both oral and literate cultures, three forms of text became possible only due to the existence of script: tables, lists, and recipes. The first two differ from the narrative in that they present items of information in a disjointed, abstracted way. To memorize a list or a table, one needs a mnemonic device to make up for the lack of connections. The recipe assumes a chronological connection and thus seems to resemble a narrative, but it lacks the propelling force of a cause or an intention—the plot of the narrative. Clouds lead to rain and greed leads to crime; sifting the flour does not lead to breaking eggs. The recipe fulfills the learning function of the narrative in that it provides the learner with a vicarious experience—but in a way that is closer to that of tables or lists. One could say that recipes are lists of actions, not objects.

Tables, lists, and recipes are undoubtedly the modern props of organizational knowledge. But if we agree with Latour (1993) that we have never become completely modern, then it can be interesting to take a look at nonmodern modes of knowing still present in contemporary organizations.

In their eager desire to be as modern (and scientific) as possible, contemporary organizations tend to ignore the role of narrative in learning, at least in their programmatic attempts to influence organizational learning. Tables and lists (many models and taxonomies are complicated lists) are given priority as teaching aids. Although tables and lists can fulfill certain functions that narratives cannot, the reverse applies even more. Almost certainly, the greater part of organizational learning happens through the circulation of stories. Also, the extent to which the modern props of learning—and the technologies of writing that support them—are used in organizations varies. My own studies of city management reveal, for example, that in the Stockholm city office many important deals are made on the phone, whereas in Warsaw every agreement has to be confirmed in writing. Stockholm, however, was flooded with leaflets, brochures, and memos, whereas in Warsaw there were very few of these and important information was conveyed face-to-face only. Oral cultures are not necessarily ages away.

Studying collective memory in nonliterate societies, Goody and Watt (1968) point out that the social function of memory—and forgetting—can thus be seen as the final stage of what may be called the homeostatic organization of the cultural tradition in non-literate society. The language is developed in intimate association with the experience of the community, and it is learned by the individual in face-to-face contact with the other members. What continues to be of social relevance is stored in the memory while the rest is usually forgotten. (pp. 30-31)

But is this something exotic, never to be met in literate societies? To begin with, as Goody and Watt (1968) note, nonliterate societies have various mnemonic techniques at their disposal. Second, the description of the non-literate community can be applied to any interpretive community in which written texts play a role secondary to that of oral or quasi-oral communication, facilitated by the modern media (telephone, the Internet). It could be said of any contemporary company that what continues to be of social relevance is stored in the memory while the rest is usually forgotten. One would only need to specify that "forgetting" means filing away, storing in an archive. As Goody and Watt observe, the oral tradition remains the primary mode of cultural orientation even in a literate culture. And the oral tradition depends on the narrative.

How does collective memory work? An answer to this question requires a return to that other operation conceived as modern and scientific but that anthropology of knowledge reveals as ancient: categorization and classification (Durkheim & Mauss, 1903/1986). Mary Douglas (1986), reviving the Durkheimian tradition, criticizes two prominent notions of social theory so crucial to organization theory: the assumption of the steady evolution of human consciousness and, consequently, of an irreparable breach between "primitive" and "modern" societies. Knowledge of the former, in face of this breach, would give no advantage for understanding the latter. Durkheim, Douglas points out, shares this assumption but luckily fails to pursue it consistently. He introduces the notion of two forms of solidarity or grounds for collective action: classification, that is, belongingness to the same group (primitive societies), and economy, that is, exchange (modern societies). Although Durkheim mourns the primitive solidarity as lost in modern societies, he nevertheless puts much effort into understanding the classificatory work performed by institutions.

When the supposed breach between primitive and modern societies is called in question (Lyotard, 1979; Latour, 1993), the work of Durkheim and Mauss (1903/1986) can be brought to bear on contemporary societies. Although the turn the collective action takes may be mainly due to economic motives, it still acquires direction from shared classifications. And although the work of classifying and negotiating classifications continues all the time in all kinds of interaction, it is facilitated and made possible by shared classifications of greater stability—the institutions. "Institutions systematically direct individual memory and channel our perceptions into forms compatible with the relations they authorize. They fix processes that are essentially dynamic, they hide their influence, and they rouse our emotions to a standardized pitch on standardized issues" (Douglas, 1986, p. 92). And, "the high triumph of institutional thinking is to make the institutions completely invisible" (p. 98). This restates what Lyotard says about scientific knowledge being legitimized by a metanarrative (of progress) and then disavowing the narrative knowledge of its legitimacy.

This effacement can be undone with no risk of a black hole of nihilism awaiting it from behind. That facts are produced (a *fact* long known to anyone who bothered to check the etymology of the word) is no reason for despair, says Karin Knorr Cetina (1994, p. 8). Modern institutions, including science, run on fictions, as all institutions always have, and the task of the scholar is to study how these fictions are constructed and sustained. A narrative approach will reveal how institutional classifications are made and will thus render the works of science more comprehensible.

> If classificatory schemes provide a science of the concrete, narrative may provide a science of the imagination. At the very least, a reemphasis on temporality may enable us to deal more directly with change, and thereby to make structural and symbolic studies more dynamic. (J. Bruner, 1986, p. 141)

This opinion is strongly supported in anthropology (Geertz, 1973, 1988), but similar claims have been made in sociology (Brown, 1977, 1980), economics (McCloskey, 1986, 1990), psychology (Gergen, 1991,1994), and history (White, 1973). But does narrative fit the genre of organization studies? Better still, does such a genre exist?

Organization Theory—A Genre?

A genre is usually conceived as a system of action that has become institutionalized and is recognizable by repetition; its meaning stems from its place within symbolic systems making up literature and culture, acquiring specificity by difference from other genres (Bruss, 1976, p. 5). Does organization theory qualify?

Organization science began as a "practical" science. When, around the turn of the century, its forefathers (plus Mary Follet) began forming the subject, they did so with the promise of solving any problems companies and administrative organizations might have. At the same time, however, this kind of knowledge was becoming a strictly academic subject, with PhDs and professors, journals, and international conferences. Organization science was thus following in the footsteps of other practical sciences such as law, medicine, and engineering.

More recently, however, other self-descriptions have come to light. In a provocative article, Astley and Zammuto (1992) claim that organization theory is nothing but a language game in its own right. If one understands this statement broadly, as a refutation of correspondence theory and an admission that all use of language is a language game, the conceptualization is convincing but does not yield much heuristic value. If, as the authors seem to suggest, one should take it more strictly as a language game played for the fun of it among a group of people closeted in academia, it loses much of its appeal and becomes rather a claustrophobic concept.

More appealing is a suggestion by Sandelands (1990), who proposes to treat theory production as a kind of practice. The product of theoretical thinking is a metaphor (see Morgan, 1986), which, although not necessarily directly connected with practice, can give the latter inspiration and evoke interesting associations, just like art does. Consequently, disciplines such as business administration and management science are academic disciplines eager to remain in close contact with practice, not with the purpose of dictating the order of things, but of reflecting and provoking via basic research and theory. Thus, the art of writing (and of speaking; the persuasive skills in general) becomes extremely important and their critical development becomes a crucial task in its own right.

It is this understanding of organization studies—as a practice, that is, a system of action that became institutionalized and recognizable—that makes the notion of organization theory analogous to that of a literary genre. After all, all that organization researchers do is read (listen) and write (speak). In that sense, Astley and Zammuto (1992) are right: Organization researchers are involved in a linguistic practice. But there is more to it than "just talking": It is important to point out that texts are actions (strictly speaking, material traces of such, but they result from action and provoke further action), and actions are texts in the sense that they must be legible to qualify as actions at all and not movements or behaviors. No "agency" is implicated in this notion of action: They are events to which intentions have been ascribed. "Action" and "text" are good metaphors for each other, but they even are more than that (Ricoeur, 1981, pp. 197-221). Actions, especially institutionalized ones, produce texts; texts not only "fix" other actions—their production and interpretation assumes actions.

Actions, to be legible, must relate to some context accessible to those who attempt to make sense of them; such a relation can be seen as a constraint. Just what such constraints and the ways of dealing with them are is well rendered in a description of a literary genre:

> All reading (or writing) involves us in choice: we choose to pursue a style or a subject matter, to struggle with or against a design. We also choose, as passive as it all may seem, to take part in an interaction, and it is here that generic labels have their use. The genre does not tell us the style or the construction of a text as much as how we should expect to "take" that style or mode of construction—what force it should have for us. And this force is derived from a kind of action that text is taken to be. (Bruss, 1976, p. 4).

The term *choice* should not mislead the reader into assuming a rational choice: What Bruss calls "a passive choice" can be also understood as following the "logic of appropriateness," as March and Olsen (1989) call the usual logic of action that aims not at the choice of an optimal alternative but at an action that will be recognized and accepted by an audience residing within the same institutional setup.

In this sense—evoking expectations by using a label—organization theory is undoubtedly a genre; perhaps, in fact, more a genre than a discipline. A useful reflection could then focus on the constraints and possibilities of this genre, how it developed in time, and its actual and potential connections to other genres.

Genre analysis, however, is often used as a classificatory device (for the most famous example, see Frye, 1957/1990). Although such a system of categories is relatively easy to construct and has a strong heuristic power, its application to concrete works is more problematic. After all, a genre is but a space within which one can position various works, and it is their vicinity or distance to other works that establishes their genre. Genre analysis in literature places most works between genres: Disagreement thus remains as to where the genre borders should run and whether it makes sense to draw them at all (Lejeune, 1989). The best-known attempt at genre analysis within organization theory, Burrell and Morgan's (1979) classification of main paradigms, reveals its heuristic power in provoking massive protests and reclassifications. One can thus envisage an alternative of creating an interpretative space that is able to contain and relate to each of many other approaches without ascribing strict positions to them. McCloskey (1986) suggests, for instance, that literary criticism can offer economics a model for self-understanding: "Literary criticism does not merely pass judgments of good or bad; in its more recent forms the question seems hardly to arise. Chiefly *it is concerned with making readers see how poets and novelists accomplish their results*" (p. xix, italics mine).

Such reflection—or self-reflection—makes a genre more distinct and more elaborate. The analysis of a genre is one of its main constitutive forces. Social scientists busy themselves constructing the institutions they describe. Describing what they do, organization researchers can increase the legitimacy of their own genre.

Not everybody is of that opinion. There are voices saying that problematizing what one does is not a good way to institutionalize it, that attracting attention to the process inevitably exposes its messiness and the lack of a priori criteria is the last thing a discipline needing legitimation wants (Pfeffer, 1993). This might be true in the case of disciplines just beginning, which are vulnerable to any doubt, but different cycles in life require different legitimation tactics. The most established disciplines such as philosophy, mathematics, or theoretical physics like nothing better than a public soul searching to renew and relegitimate themselves. This is helped by the fact that the very attempt to define a genre, as Lejeune (1989) points out, is paradoxical: It can be done only by exploring the gray zones and borderline cases. Genres blur as soon as you look at them at close range.

Neither paradoxicality nor the presence of conflict needs to debilitate a field; on the contrary, they enhance its controlling power. Institutions emerge and renew themselves "by generating just the right kind of tension or even conflict, creative rather than destructive" (MacIntyre, 1981/1990, p. 171). Delineating borders facilitates transgressions, stabilizing them provides a basis for experimentation, routinizing them unleashes creativity. As language renews itself via paradox (Lyotard, 1979/1986), so social practices renew themselves via tensions and contradictions. The narrative approach can thus also be seen as a loan from literary theory that will problematize organization theory, thus enabling it to reinvigorate itself.

Narrative in and on Organizations

Narrative enters organization studies in at least four forms: organizational research that is written in a storylike fashion ("tales from the field," to paraphrase Van Maanen, 1988); organizational research that collects organizational stories (tales of the field); organizational research that conceptualizes organizational life as story making and organization theory as story reading (interpretative approaches); and a disciplinary reflection that takes the form of literary critique.

Narrative forms of organization studies are easiest to find in case studies: research cases, educational cases, and fictive cases that use chronology as the main organizing device. One interesting example is Robin Leidner's (1993) *Fast Food, Fast Talk*. Leidner studies the process of service work with the help of two cases, McDonald's and Combined Insurance, and offers the readers two narratives elucidating along theoretical, nonnormative lines a viable way of combining narrative with the logico-scientific mode of reporting.

Another interesting use of narrative can be found in the case teaching method that consciously exploits the structure of narrative. Students are given the first element of a plot and the third element is implied as a reverse of the first. Their task is to fill in the second element, that is, the action. The case concentrates on a detailed description of the original state that must contain the cues for how to reverse it. The status of the case is halfway between fact and fiction: It is assumed that the case originated in actual research but it is also taken for granted that the description is heavily stylized to satisfy the demands of the classroom.

Bearing this in mind, one finds it less surprising that novels are used as cases in teaching management. Literary texts appear on the reading lists of management schools. *Harvard Business Review* encourages its readers to "read fiction to the bottom line" to find managerial wisdom (DeMott, 1989, p. 128), a suggestion that was formulated long before by Dwight Waldo (1968). Yet another possibility is to provide readers with close readings of novels from the starting point of organizational analysis (Czarniawska-Joerges & Guillet de Monthoux, 1994; Phillips, 1995). Although students of organizations no doubt will profit enormously from reading novels themselves, there is an extension of the space of shared meanings that more focused readings can offer: the explicit connection between the narrative and the logico-scientific mode of knowing.

As for the second way of introducing narrative into organization studies, that is, collecting stories from the organization floor, it started with the works of Clark (1972) and Mitroff and Kilmann (1975). Organizational stories became a legitimate topic of organization studies only in the 1980s and are exemplified in the works of Martin and her collaborators (e.g., Martin, 1982; Martin, Hatch, & Sitkin, 1983).

Stories from the field were at first treated analytically by field researchers. Recently, however, they have been increasingly retold in a slightly stylized way in the belief that such stories can teach students the practices of the field much more successfully than texts written in a scientific mode. In this context, at least two examples, both focusing on Anglo Saxon organizations, are worth mentioning: Frost, Mitchell, and Nord (1978 and subsequent editions), and Sims, Gabriel, and Fineman (1993).

Many well-known studies from the 1980s, as pointed out by Boland and Tankasi (1995), conceived of organizational narratives as artifacts forever petrified in organizational reality out there waiting to be collected. With time, however, the convention grew broader as it began to include other attempts such as Boje's (1991), Boland's (1989, 1994), Forester's (1992), and Gabriel's (1995)—all of which accentuated the process of story telling as the never-ending construction of meaning in organizations. Weick (1995) made this the focus of his most recent book.

Although much of organizational life is spent reading stories already made and interpreting them within a set of already existing rules (routines), sensemaking or the activity of attributing meaning to previously meaningless cues also occurs. Weick (1995) explores seven properties of organizational sensemaking: identity, retrospect, enactment, social contact, ongoing events, cues, and plausibility. After discussing plausibility (which in organizational practice is much more important than accuracy—the fetish of perception studies), Weick summarizes the most important aspects of sensemaking:

> If accuracy is nice but not necessary in sensemaking, than what is necessary? The answer is, something that preserves plausibility and coherence, something that is reasonable and memorable, something that embodies past experience and expectations, something which resonates with other people, something that can be constructed retrospectively but also can be used prospectively, something that captures both feeling and thought, something that allows for embellishment to fit current oddities, something that is fun to contrast. In short, what is necessary in sensemaking is a good story. (pp. 60-61)

This, in Weick's opinion, is what is most needed "in an equivocal, postmodern world, infused with the politics of interpretation and conflicting interests" (p. 61). This is consistent with the postulate of requisite variety, known from his earlier work, suggesting that complex objects must be met by complex models (Weick, 1979). Although stories simplify the world and are therefore useful as guides for action, they simplify it less than the kind of formal models that used to be revered as genuine science.

Weick's (1995) perspective can be counted among interpretive approaches to organization studies. This tradition of organization studies—mentioned by Burrell and Morgan (1979) and made distinct by Putnam and Pacanowsky (1983), Lincoln (1985), and Jones, Moore, and Snyder (1988)—can be said to be truly established. Although the approach is somewhat differently cut, most of the contributions in books dedicated to organizational symbolism (Pondy, Frost, Morgan, & Dandridge, 1983; B. A. Turner, 1990) are of interpretive persuasion. Most works, although not all, in the organizational culture tradition lean toward the interpretive side (Frost et al., 1985; Frost, Moore, Louis, Lundberg, & Marten, 1991). An anthology dedicated to organizational artifacts (Gagliardi, 1990) presents an array of interpretive approaches, although it also hosts noninterpretive contributions. The point of all these efforts, however, is not to come up with an improved story from the field but with alternative or competitive stories to engage in a dialogue with the field. Weick's perspective can be applied on yet another level: research as sensemaking.

The efforts of researchers as sensemakers must be interpreted again: Thus, we come to yet another fit between the narrative approach and texts of organization theory, a fit that expresses itself as a kind of literary critique. This was attempted first by John Van Maanen (1988). Although his tales of the field are focused not on organization studies only but on ethnographies in general, his work can be said to have legitimized the literary kind of reflection within the discipline. Sandelands and Drazin (1989), Sandelands (1990), Astley and Zammuto (1992), and Sköldberg (1992) began a debate on organization theory language, audience, and the criterion of "goodness" that still continues. I have attempted a genre analysis (1997b), which carries inspiration from Van Maanen (1988) and McCloskey (1990) into organization studies. Golden-Biddle and Locke (1993) analyze textual strategies employed in organizational ethnographies. The hope is that thanks to those excursions into the narrative, organization studies will be able to appreciate everyday organizational knowledge and to become more skillful in crafting their own narratives.

Organizational narratives, as the main mode of knowing and communicating in organizations, are an important focus for organization researchers. Their construction and reproduction must be documented and their contents must be interpreted. Narrative forms of reporting will enrich organization studies themselves, complementing, illustrating, and scrutinizing logico-scientific forms of reporting. By relinquishing some aspirations to power through the claim of factuality and one-to-one correspondence of theory and the world, organization studies can open their texts for negotiation and thus enter in a dialogical relationship with organizational practice.

To do this, it is not enough just to tell stories. It is necessary to establish the provenience of the story: Is this a story told in the field? If so, in whose formulation is it quoted here? The rendition of the researcher-observer? The verbatim quote of an organizational actor? In which situations is the story told? Helmers and Buhr (1994) report the story of a "buxomly secretary" that was told to them as ethnographers by several interlocutors but was also, as it turned out, printed in the in-house publication of the company they studied as early as 30 years before. The story is a tale of a clumsy female and a skillful mechanic, and was generally treated as an exemplification of a "historical" fact of women's incapacity of dealing with new technologies, which supposedly hampered the introduction of electric typewriter technology.

In the case of the story of the engineer and the failed promotion, which was formulated on the basis of an observation from the field, the story was put into the form of the minimal narrative for the purpose of presenting it to a specific group of readers—students of business, management, and related disciplines. We used the narrative to enter into a dialogue with a specific field of practice—R&D company—that resides in between our own (university research and teaching) and the one the students learn about (business and administration organizations). The economy of the narrative was intentional; the minimal form was to ensure maximal ambiguity, and therefore interpretative flexibility. Readers' comments were in turn interpreted according to a hermeneutic triad (see Chapter 5, " Doing the Reading and Doing the Writing: From the Field to the Text").

A self-reflective reading can be attempted, but I feel that after Ashmore (1989), not much new can be achieved by following this direction. The critique is best done by others. The interpretation of various readings of the failed promotion narrative is reported in Czarniawska and Calàs (in press). It is important to stress, however, that my use of the narrative device is neither a model nor a blueprint but just an example. The device is everybody's to use, reconstruct, and deconstruct at will.

Theater der Exoten (Paul Klee, 1922)

2 IS THERE A METHOD IN THIS STUDY?
Anthropology as a Frame of Mind

The narrative device does not predetermine in any sense how the material is to be constructed or collected. In more traditional parlance, there is no obvious connection between the narrative approach and any specific method of study. It is doubtful whether there is any method in social science studies, at least in the sense of a prescribed procedure, that brings about foreseeable results. There is a bunch of institutionalized practices on the one hand and individual experimentation accompanied by self-reflection on the other. An adherent to any approach, including the narrative one, must create a fit between her or his worldview and the accessible (or inevitable) practices. By definition, such fits are potentially many, although only some will become institutionalized and widely spread. Here I present one such fit—between the narrative approach and anthropology as a way of collecting and constructing narratives in fieldwork. In the context of organization research, such studies should be properly called *anthropologically inspired* in deference to rules and procedures of a discipline that I intend, in the words of Michel de Certau (1984), to poach rather than observe.

Why Do Fieldwork?

Organizational narratives abound. It is not even necessary to go to the library or buy a newspaper to collect them. I receive by mail annual reports of several companies to which I am but vaguely connected: Scandinavian Airlines, an insurance company, a housing cooperative. Global economies are at my fingertips on Netscape. What kind of misplaced romanticism attracts me to "the field"?

First, it is in the field that one can study the actual *production* of narratives. Before a glossy brochure reaches my mailbox, there has been a long discussion about which accounting data to include, what tone the CEO's letter should strike. Like sociologists of science who go to laboratories to see how facts are manufactured (Latour & Woolgar, 1979/1986; Knorr Cetina, 1981), organization scholars go to the field to see how organizations are produced.

My remarks on narrative production might raise anxiety among those who suspect that all language-interested approaches are idealist. Surely organizations produce more than narratives? Surely annual reports are neither the only nor the most important products?

Organizations reproduce themselves and produce things, services, social relations, and organizational actors. They also produce economic facts (an observation that seems to escape many sociologists of science, who are bravely questioning natural science but are in awe of economics). Global economy is produced locally. But all these local products must be connected into a meaningful whole. Although statistics and lists of categories are some of the ways of such connection, the narrative is the dominant one. This is what I mean by production of narratives: the process of association, of building the "and, and, and" connections between actions and events and negotiating them with the readers.

Moreover, collecting narratives from a safe place at a university erases that part of the insight offered by MacIntyre (1981/1990) that speaks of social life as an *enacted* narrative. In fact, there used to be a rift between scholars fond of narrative metaphors and those who prefer theater metaphors. This rift probably goes back to the early uses of theater metaphors in the Goffmanian sense: the notions of backstage and front stage, the notions of make-believe as contrasted to reality. But even Goffman (1974) moved away from these dichotomies to an idea that the difference between make-believe and reality is a fluid one and so is the difference between theater and real life. It is therefore heartening to see the increasing number of works that emphatically join the two (e.g., Turner, W. W., & E. M. Bruner, 1986). Every novel contains a potential script; every narrative waits to be enacted. Organizational narratives are both inscriptions of past performances and scripts and staging instructions for future performances.

Another reason for going to the field is because it is there that narratives abound. Of the many narratives produced in the field, its representatives send me one, having decided that this one is good for me as their client. As a student of their mores, I might want to use a different selection principle. I might select, for instance, narratives that they wish to hide from me or that they themselves consider important for internal use.

People in the field of practice produce narratives and consume a multitude of narratives produced elsewhere. Their selection procedures are of obvious interest to an organization student, and it is equally obvious that it is easier to figure these out by observation than by speculation. What do they read and why?

I would like to emphasize, however, that my preference for fieldwork does not have much to do with empiricism. It can be seen as opposite of the traditional empiricism with its motto *nullius in verba* (on no man's word) because the words of men and women in the field are as valid as my own. If fieldwork must be seen as empirical, I would call this type of empiricism *ethical*. Richard Rorty (1982) puts it very well when he says,

> [it is] a mistake to think of somebody's own account of his behavior or culture as epistemically privileged. He might have a good account of what he is doing or he might not, but it is *not* a mistake to think of it as morally privileged. We have a duty to listen to his account, not because he has privileged access to his own motives but because he is a human being like ourselves. (p. 202)

The field is where "the Other" lives. Thus, to me, fieldwork is an expression of curiosity of the Other, about people who construct their worlds differently from the way I construct mine.

As is often the case, a metaphoric example can convey the message with much more strength than lengthy discussions can. I stress my point by using an illustration taken from a well-known novel by David Lodge (1988) called *Nice Work*. The story told in the novel catches the very essence of anthropological work—its promises and traps alike. At the same time, it describes a unique instance of a truly symmetric anthropology where the studied becomes the student.

Robyn, a postfeminist and a poststructuralist academic, lives in a two-dimensional world: the world of symbols and politics (the latter in both the positive sense of the feminist movement and the negative sense of the politics of academia). Prompted by the politics of academia, she enters another world—that of industry. Her counterpart in that world—the managing director Vic—lives similarly in a two-dimensional world: the political and the practical one. Symbols do not exist for Vic; practical things do not exist for Robyn.

Robyn is determined to make her visit a nonanthropological one. She plans to colonize the other world, taking for granted that her world contains all the concepts and tools needed to dismantle the other. For Vic, Robyn's visit is an intrusion that has to be tolerated (for political reasons), but he has no fear of colonization. Vic takes his world to be the only correct one: He takes it for granted. Thus, Robyn's feelings of superiority: As a poststructuralist, she knows better than that. Or so she thinks—Lodge is showing us that, although Robyn relativizes Victor's world, she takes her own world for granted just like Victor does.

Lodge opens his book with a quote from Disraeli (*Sybil; or, the Two Nations*):

> Two nations; between whom there is no intercourse and no sympathy; who are as ignorant of each other's habits, faults and feelings, as if they were dwellers in different zones, or inhabitants of different planets; who are formed by a different breeding, and fed by different food, and ordered by different manners . . . (Lodge, 1988, p. 8)

This quote summarizes the author's and possibly the reader's perspective. The two characters do not see themselves as belonging to different worlds: They are inhabitants of the same country in the same time. Their professions differ, but surely people from different professions can live together in close symbiosis. The encounter proves to be a shock to both of them, the realization—at first accompanied by negative feelings—of the completeness and strangeness of the other world, then curiosity, and finally mutual learning and respect.

The result of their encounter is that each remains in his or her own appropriate world, but this world is enriched, with a new dimension added that, although it adapts uneasily, cannot be conveniently forgotten or removed. Victor enters the world of symbols and will never again see the ad for Silk Cut cigarettes with naive eyes. Robyn will live with a memory of hell—the foundry that she visited will replace her image of industries straight from the Victorian novels.

There is also a political point to the story. Vic's insistence on exchanging roles—he becomes an anthropologist and visits the university—completes the experience by reinterpreting Robyn's world. This experience is not unknown but is rare in the annals of anthropology—that natives visit researchers at their home base. A fictionalized (or rather "scientifized") description of complications it produces can be found in Tama Janowitz's (1987) *A Cannibal in Manhattan*. There are several—partly apocryphic—stories of this kind describing the beginnings of anthropology, but the topic cannot be safely historicized. An anthropological study of a Danish village was made by an Indian anthropologist (Prakash, 1991) and a TV documentary on "contemporary Germans" was done by Turkish anthropologists, which showed, among other things, that rich Germans hunt their meat, whereas the poor buy it at a supermarket. The "natives" were moderately amused that every world can be reinterpreted and pulled inside out. A truly symmetric anthropology consists not in "being nice to the natives" but in allowing the researchers to be anthropologized in turn.

Lodge's (1988) characters are forced, by a turn of events, to become both anthropologists, and anthropologists' subjects, and what they learn from this somewhat unsettling experience is exactly that which, one hopes, will crown the efforts of anthropologists in general:

> An enlargement of the possibility of intelligible discourse between people quite different from one another in interest, outlook, wealth, and power and yet contained in a world in which, tumbled as they are into endless connection, it is increasingly difficult to get out of each other's way. (Geertz, 1988, p. 147)

I need to point out that Lodge's (1988) characters sin against at least two golden rules of traditional anthropology: They do fieldwork within the same (national) culture and they do not make a prolonged study as participant-observers. I suggest that their vices are to be made into virtues, even if this might mean that anthropology is being poached in the interest of organization studies.

Anthropology and Complex Organizations

One of the assumptions firmly held within anthropology is that field research within one's own society invariably sanctions an unquestioning attitude in which meanings and their modes of construction are taken for granted by the researchers. Leach (1985), for example, "at the cost of being accused of being old-fashioned," is against the idea of anthropology at home:

> Field work in a cultural context of which you already have intimate first-hand experience seems to be much more difficult than field work which is approached from the naive viewpoint of a total stranger. When anthropologists study facets of their own society their vision seems to be distorted by prejudices which derive from private rather than public experience. (Leach, 1982, p. 124)

As the controversy over Margaret Mead's studies has shown, there is a good reason to suspect that these "prejudices" usually accompany the anthropologist to exotic countries (Toulmin, 1984). On the other hand, many researchers find professional practices other than their own almost as exotic as the mores of the Trobrianders (Sanday, 1979). Desensitization or bias must be weighed against the clumsy ignorance of the outsider, which can be removed only by complete acculturation—if such is possible:

> Such nonsense has been written, by people who should know better, about the anthropologists "being accepted." It is sometimes suggested that an alien people will somehow come to view the visitor of distinct race and culture as in every way similar to the locals. This is, alas, unlikely. The best one could probably hope for is to be viewed as a harmless idiot who brings certain advantages to this village. (Barley, 1986, p. 56)

Nigel Barley deserves to be a patron saint of anthropologically inspired organization studies. He helped demystify the anthropological procedure, showing anthropologists as pathetic figures, dupes in alien cultures, whose heroism came from overcoming the hardship and absurdity of their situation, not from the superiority of their knowledge or their stance (Barley, 1983, 1988). Against the judgment of his elders, Barley claims that it makes sense to study one's own culture; he received vindication in the form of a BBC series (*Native Land,* 1989).

Many of Barley's observations apply not only to studies of villages but also to studies of corporations. In these, the natives may sometimes briefly nurse the illusion of sharing a common culture with the visiting researchers ("You as an economist must surely see that . . ."), but these tender and ephemeral illusions do not eliminate the irreducible sense of strangeness. With luck, the visitor may be regarded as an uninformed but well-meaning researcher—a euphemism for a harmless idiot or a nuisance. Anthropological tales from the field sometimes frame the researcher as the fool, but it seems to me that the role of the fool, so close to the trickster and other seemingly harmless but actually powerful figures, is aspired to, and perhaps given to, men. A woman may choose between being just silly or simply being uninformed.

I take up the problems connected with such positioning in the field and the threats it presents to researchers' identity in the next chapter. At present, I return to some other anthropological rules that become broken or bent in organization studies. One such rule concerns a necessity for a prolonged period of participant observation. This rule encounters four problems in research practice: participation, time, space, and invisibility.

Severyn Bruyn once said that "the method of the social scientist . . . must take dramatic account of the social cultural world—the complex of actors and their plots as they live and dream on the stage of society" (1976, p. xiv). Research techniques that help grasp the social drama as it appears to the actors, their views of their roles, and their assumptions about the unfolding plot are needed. The most obvious way of doing this is, in Bruyn's opinion, participant observation. In the case of organization research, this means that the researcher assumes the role of an organizational member or the other way around—an employee becomes a researcher. This is the method adopted by Melville Dalton (1959, who worked as a manager), Michael Burawoy (1979, machine-tool operator), John Van Maanen (1982, police trainee), and Robin Leidner (1993, McDonald's worker and Combined Insurance trainee).

These examples indicate that such studies—no doubt superior to all other types—are possible to carry out either due to exceptional luck in obtaining access or because a given working place does not require specific qualifications. But even the latter requires some luck or special dispositions. I could not possibly work as a radium drill operator, and my only factory job—in a fruit preservative factory—was brought to an abrupt end by a dramatic stomach indisposition after having eaten too much fruit. Perhaps I could manage to act as a personnel manager, but with such an effort that it would effectively prevent me from observing. It would take me years to obtain the state of "detached involvement" that Bruyn (1966) declares to be the ideal state for a participant-observer when dropped in the midst of an alien culture. A participant observation of a dance differs from a participant observation in a top management emergency meeting. It is necessary to emphasize, however, that I use the term *participant observation* literally, which does not include direct observation (Schwartzman, 1993), that is, a situation in which the researcher is present but as an observer, not as a participant. Direct observation is an obvious possibility for organization students and it gains in potential if the time of observation is prolonged. This is not to say that longer is better.

The issue of time is problematic in organization studies in more than one sense. Consider, for example, the advice that Sharon Traweek (1992) gives to her colleagues, science researchers, in her otherwise beautifully ironic and informative article on narrative strategies in science studies:

> Our first field work should last a minimum of one year, preferably two; subsequent field trips can last as little as three months and as long as they occur at least every three or four years. The questions and theories change, but we study the same people if they survive as a community, and maybe later on we also study some of their neighbors. (p. 438)

My study of the management of the city of Warsaw (Czarniawska, in press) took me about 14 months, 4 of which were directly in the field. During that time, a new city council was elected, which meant that I lost half of my interlocutors. Moreover, the neighbors also changed as a result of an administrative reform. The point is that I was not studying a community of city managers but an *action net* of city management: interconnected acts of organizing.

Another way of stating this contrast is to use an opposition introduced by, among others, Berger and Luckmann (1995)—a community of life versus a community of meaning. Whereas the first can be located in a concrete point in time and space and observed on the spot, the latter—like Mary Douglas's thought world—is more or less deduced by a researcher who traces connections and common action patterns. Communities of meaning can be, in organization theory terms, constructed as professions or organization fields. Such a move, however, requires and admits an active construction of such a field, whereas studying a community or an organization assumes its prior existence. Of course, there is no completely neutral starting point and every researcher takes something for granted (if only the existence of a language in which the report is to be written). It is the purpose of the study that makes the difference and sets the starting point. Following Latour's (1994) appeal that we should explain such phenomena as power and structure rather than use them as explanations, I wish to catch structures and identities in forming. I start with a network of action because this starting point seems to be early enough to permit studying the process by which organizations, actors, and structures are constructed. This means that I take for granted that, in the world I know, production is connected to sales, which are connected to marketing (thus forming a net of action). Such an action net is an expression of an existing institutional order. Within that order, however, action nets take up different and similar patterns, new practices become institutionalized and old ones become sedimented, borders are delineated and fought about, identities are formulated and reformulated—and this is what I want to study. Going back to the origins of existing action nets would require a span of at least 200 years and a global presence—in other words, another type of study that does not permit a direct fieldwork.

Traweek (1992) has studied Japanese physicists for 20 years now and she feels that she is beginning to get the gist of their lives and activities. Suppose I study the Warsaw management for 20 more years. It would no doubt be a fascinating study, but I wonder whether there will be much in the management of Warsaw in 2015 that is of crucial importance for understanding management of that city in 1995. Persons might retire or become exchanged as the result of the next political coup, but the actions that constitute management will remain; on the other hand, the actions' form and content might change drastically even if the same people remain as a result of new information technology or a new fashion in big-city management. There is no essence that I might reveal in time. I think that Traweek was misled by the fact that Japanese physicists seem to be a community of meaning that is very close to a community of life.

In such a case, Traweek's would be an illusion of stability caused by a coincidence in space. Another possibility is that it has to do with that which Fabian (1983) sees as a habit in anthropology: counting the time of the Other in a different way than our time is counted. I will simplify Fabian's complex argument by mentioning two such differences: The Other's time goes slowly, and it is not coeval (the Other is perceived as living in another era). Time in contemporary complex organizations is condensed and it is counted at many places concurrently. It is not only coeval but multiple. Studying such organizations might thus help remove this time prejudice from anthropological studies, but this is Fabian's (and anthropologists') business.

My research tasks will be met more effectively not by prolonging my fieldwork but by studying the management of other big cities at the same time (which I am attempting to do). Such a move, however, reveals another difficulty resulting from an attempt to follow the anthropological tradition: that of dealing with space. Traditional anthropology can be seen as a product of the 19th century, whose great obsession, Foucault (1980) says, was history, "with its themes of development and of suspension, of crisis and cycle, themes of the ever accumulating past. . . . Space was treated as the dead, the fixed, the undialectical, the immobile. Time, on the contrary, was richness, fecundity, life, dialectical" (p. 70). The present epoch, he adds, may turn into an epoch of space and simultaneous networks.

Unfortunately, an observer is usually situated—in one room, one corridor, one branch—although some "excursions" may happen, especially when a shadowing technique is used. Modern organizing, on the other hand, takes place in a net of fragmented, multiple contexts through multitudes of kaleidoscopic movements. Thus, the well-settled traditional observer might end up leading the life of the medieval peasant among modern city folks.

Time, Space, (In)Visibility

These, then, are the challenges of time and space that the contemporary organization student has to tackle: Organizing happens in many places at once and organizers move around quickly and a lot. Moreover, many of their activities are intellectual and therefore unobservable, as everybody who ever tried to observe a person working a computer well knows.

One of the ways I try to tackle those difficulties is by *shadowing*—a technique compiled from such disparate sources as Truman Capote (put to use in the social sciences by Sclavi, 1989) and Henry Mintzberg (1979). Capote (1972) followed a black cleaning woman during one day of her duties. Sclavi followed Italian and U.S. high school students in their daily school activities. Mintzberg followed top managers. I follow selected interlocutors in their everyday work for a period of about 10 working days. This allows me to move with them and to move from one point in an action net to another because I am after not individual experience but a collective construction.

This technique, however, does not tackle the issues of simultaneity and invisibility, and so additional techniques must be considered. One of them is what I call *observant participation,* a method I proposed and introduced in a study of a consumer goods management system in Poland (Czarniawska, 1980). The study was carried out in several stages. In each stage, actors (10 to 25 at a time) in chosen organizations and under our guidance collected systematic observations of events over a period of 18 months. It must be pointed out that it would have been impossible to insert up to 25 researchers as observers into organizations in the same branch. Were it possible, they would have had to wait some time to become acculturated enough to be able to start their observations. This would defy the aim of the research, which must be condensed. Nine years later, these organizations ceased to exist. Organizations are institutionalized action nets, not groups of people and not communities, although they for periods of time might behave as such.

I still use the observant participation approach whenever I can because it has proved fruitful (Czarniawska, 1997a). It is a variation of *ethnographic interviews* (Spradley, 1979), that is, repetitive, open, and extensive interviews aimed at achieving an account of people's work and organizations. Another variation is what I call *narrative interviews*: chronological relations of events that occurred under a specified period of time. Although it is impossible to start a study with a narrative interview ("Hello. Please tell me what happened at your unit the last 2 weeks"), narrative interviews become a natural development in serial interviewing, which usually starts with a thematically focused interview. What I find attractive in narrative interviews is that both the structure (the plot) and the main concepts (metaphors) are chosen by the interlocutor rather than the researcher. Even more important, these interviews relate actual, not generalized, events ("How do you make decisions?") or hypothetical events ("What would you do if . . .?"). In that, they come near to an everyday account and therefore to direct observation.

After all, as John Law (1994) points out, nothing ever happens right where and when the researcher is observing. All important events happen at some other time, other place. Although in the beginning researchers tend to be taken by panic and try to chase "the action," in time they learn that important events are made into such in accounts. Nobody is aware that an important event is happening when it takes place, although some writers exploit the reader's credulity by inserting sentences such as "I felt distinctly that something crucial was about to take place."

The mistrust of interviews as a field technique within the anthropological method is very serious. Interviews gained their bad reputation due to a misapprehension of the kind of material they produce (see also Silverman, 1993). Typically, the interview material is seen as transparent, as a window to something else: "Now I know how they make strategic decisions!" This is deceptive: Now I know (only) how they account for their strategic decision making. Although most talk is about something other than itself, it represents nothing but itself. But that is not a little. Although an interview provides what Van Maanen (1988) calls "representational data," "doing representations" is an important part of organizing and therefore plays an operational function. There is no reason to suspect that the researcher's organizational interlocutors are staging a completely new, unique representational mode just for the benefit of one researcher. If so, unlikely as it might be, it would be easy to discover it in the next interview with another interlocutor. I am sure that a whole company staging a coherent performance just for one researcher extends anybody's will to suspend disbelief.

But what if I want to know how managers make strategic decisions, not how they account for them? There are several hidden assumptions in this question that I will try to uncloak one by one. First, let me try to answer this question semantically, that is, literally. I can interview several people who, to my knowledge, participate in strategic decision making. Isn't that the way to learn about what is common in their way of accounting? Certainly, but this shared element in their accounts is important; it is an inscription of the organizing that went into producing it.

I can also observe meetings in which, managers claim, strategic decisions are made. Again, this will not tell me how decisions are *really* made. I will just be able to add one more account—mine. The main advantage of this approach is that it is what De Vault (1990) calls a *novel reading*—an account from a person that is not socialized into the same system of meaning, but is familiar enough with it to recognize it as such (deciding what is strategic decision making is not exactly telling gray round pebbles from white square ones). It may thus vary from a standard account of the same event and because of this bring in new insights—a "meaning added" and a second, semiotic reading of the innocent question posed at the outset. The question "But what do they actually *do*?" betrays a belief in the possibility of a direct access to reality, in a superior knowledge, probably coming via the senses (as sense data, the empiricist's equivalent of the alchemist's stone). Braved by a constructivist reflection, I know that no such thing is possible and it does not worry me much. I do interviews to elicit standard accounts of a practice of interest to me. I do observations to contrast these accounts with nonstandard ones (novel readings) and to use the gap between the two as a source of knowledge. Observation is always a kind of garfinkeling, as the activity of breaking the implicit rules of conduct is called in honor of the ethnomethodologist Harold Garfinkel, and in this way cognitively milking the "taken for granted" of everyday life. A conclusion must therefore be that there is no dramatic difference between the material collected via observations and the material collected via interviews, that they complement one another and ought in turn to be complemented by many other techniques.

The attractiveness of all such techniques needs to be measured against the degree to which they permit one to tackle the peculiarities of modern organizing: the condensed time, the simultaneity of events taking place in different settings, and the invisibility of a growing part of operations.

The next step will no doubt lead us to a whole new set of problems—and solutions—of and in cyberspace. Traditional observation may become impossible or, on the contrary, it will be possible to the extent that no interviews will ever be needed. Before this happens, though, the actual (as contrasted with the virtual) presence in the field is in itself a source of problems.

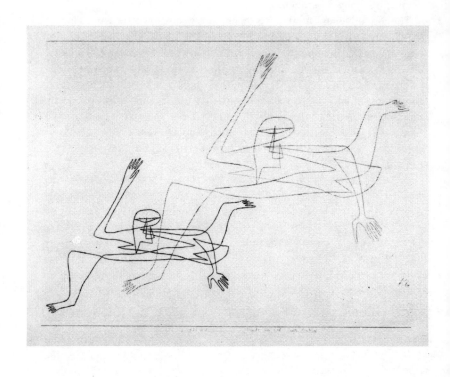

Flucht vor sich (Paul Klee, 1931)

3 POSITIONING IN THE FIELD, OR THE OTHER AS MYSELF

Doing fieldwork is in many ways like moving into an alien culture. Field-workers have to undergo enculturation, a process that is experienced as painful because it is a question of acculturation: Researchers are not *tabula rasa* but members of another culture. During such a process, the identity of the researchers—that image of themselves that successfully functioning adults take for granted—is challenged. Also, although it is less acute in fieldwork, the sense of "being dumb," of continually running up against blank walls, implies something of a confrontation with an alien culture.

Such aspects are rarely taken up in reflection on access problems. It is assumed that access is a process that ends when the collection of material in the field actually begins, a process of seeking access that precedes the moment of securing it. Difficulties in securing formal permission to do a study can be formidable and in some extreme cases can produce the only story there is (G. Bonazzi, personal communication, April 4, 1995; Rottenburg, 1995). I argue, however, that seeking access continues throughout the whole study, that there is no such felicitous moment when the study can continue without hindrance. This trait might spring from specific characteristics of organization studies as compared with other kinds of fieldwork, for instance, the mobility of the study objects and thus the necessity of the mobility of the researcher and the existence of a symmetrical relationship between the researching and the researched subjects.

These difficulties, mentioned in the previous chapter, intensify in the kind of approach I am advocating here. Studying action nets means that access secured in one organization does not suffice; several organizations are involved in an action net. Delivering water and disposing of sewage requires connections between construction, engineering, software production, laboratory work, and financial controls, to name but a few actions within

33

the net. In a sense, classical organization studies such as those in the Tavistock tradition (e.g., Jaques, 1951; Rice, 1958/1987) are more similar to community studies of the kind discussed by Traweek (1992)—either because the organizing process is different (less fragmented, less dispersed) or because the way to approach it is different. Studies of action nets create multiple access situations that require a multitude of cover stories; access is never secured once and for all but is always precarious, in need of constant maintenance; the multiple thresholds contribute to a feeling that there is no "inside" where researchers can safely reside but merely a series of antechambers, where being inside one is outside of another.

This is not to say that problems of this kind are new and specific to contemporary organizations and their researchers. A collection of access stories in organization studies by Brown, Guillet de Monthoux, and McCullough (1976), inspired by Kaplan (1964), seeks to reveal the tacit dimensions of research practices. Among the stories from the field, one is told by a U.K. scholar, Nigel Nicholson, about negotiating research in industrial relations, where access had to be obtained simultaneously from management and from unions. Nicholson's conclusion is,

> I suppose I feel that in situations like these people are less interested in precisely what you want to do than what sort of person you are: whether you will put people's backs up, that you are trustworthy, not a left-wing infiltrator, that you are impartial, that you are not an idiot. The details of your programme tend only to be a major concern when you are on some specific problem solving exercise. (Brown et al., 1976, p. 93)

The main gist of Nicholson's (Brown et al., 1976) account is that both parties—management and unions—follow their routine interaction patterns throughout, whereby the researcher's access becomes a bargaining issue. Nicholson almost left the field before learning not to take routine cues too literally and understanding that the content of his study was not an issue—his study was.

I selected this quotation because it implicitly assumes what cannot be assumed in all cases, that is, that the researchers, the managers, and the stewards are all made of the same clay, that they are able to estimate each other's trustworthiness and political allegiances. In many cases, where the researcher is a woman or a foreigner and thus an alien, this would not work. Charles McMillan (in Brown et al., 1976) found it easier doing research in Japan than in Britain, although on rather strange grounds:

> There was a certain fascination in having a Canadian coming from Britain and someone from an American university to study their companies. The Japanese

were curious to know what we wanted to study and they had an appreciation of the distance we had come. They felt, too, that we were legitimizing a kind of research that other countries undertook and Japan did not do and, therefore, they not only wanted it done but have seen it to be done. In terms of managerial issues, I don't think they were all that optimistic that we were going to give them really practical suggestions about how to improve anything. (Brown et al., 1976, pp. 137-138)

All in all the accounts collected in Brown et al., (1976), interesting as they are, are somewhat defective on the narrative side because they lack detail and complexity. Part of the explanation is that the editors of the book ask a general question—How are access problems solved and perceived by practical investigators?—and usually receive a general answer, sometimes with concrete illustrations. Another part of the explanation is that when the book was written, self-reflection was not as a rule included in research reports and books. Once secured, access was not a point to dwell on when reporting study results.

Other times and other places produce other mores. My impression is that access issues were more openly discussed in anthropology. Women were never properly enculturated into the male fields and were especially prone to talk about the never-ending process of renegotiating their presence in the field (Wax, 1971; Golde, 1986). Similarly, young researchers experience more difficulties, and are more transparent in their field stories than their more experienced colleagues, as can be seen from the following descriptions of "My worst day in the field," written by doctoral students on my request.[1]

Dangers of the Field

The first account concerns a visit to a truly exotic place.

STRANGE STORIES OF MY ADVENTUROUS LIFE

It was my first day in Budapest, in the city summer heat. I had an appointment scheduled with the director of Western Electronics in Hungary, an impressive and busy Herr Doktor who had nevertheless given me a slot for an interview in our brief telephone conversation. Now, half an hour before our meeting, I was standing in my suit and tie, in an East European streetcar, exchanging stares with my fellow travelers. As I carefully traced the advance of the streetcar on my city map, I felt the tiredness of a sleepless night coming over me. A new city, a new apartment, a new interview. I had arrived the day before and a good friend had given me a guided tour of the city. Western Electronics was located on the outskirts, whereas I lived downtown. But the streetcars were a reliable means of transportation. My friend helped me to locate the yellow streetcar track on the map. It was supposed to pass right by the street I wanted.

Now I was standing here, holding on to the handle as we slowly left downtown. Colorful sequences of images passed by, the brown Danube, roads swarming with small East European cars, beautifully decorated house fronts still bearing the marks of war damage, street signs with the names crossed over, plane trees along the street. It was like seeing scenes from a picturesque movie. But after a while, the road and sidewalks became filthy and rough. The streetcar passed by housing areas that looked like barracks, row after row of dilapidated yellow tenements. Children with grimy faces were running around, the women seemed to be on their way to some strenuous cleaning or industrial jobs. There were some men sitting around a table with wine bottles, playing cards.

I looked at my watch. It was 20 to 9, and the streetcar had barely idled its way over two thirds of the distance. The car turned alongside a graveyard and came to a three-way crossroads. To my alarm, I noticed that the yellow track on the map split two ways, and I had missed it. I didn't know which way my streetcar was turning, I held my breath and heaved a sigh of relief as it turned "my way." The car inched its way past another row of barracks and a couple of broad streets with heavy traffic. I asked one of the passengers about my stop. There it was, a bit further down the street. It was a big junction for streetcars, buses, and the subway along the wide street "ut Kerepsi."

I was standing with my map in the middle of the morning rush, with people swarming in all directions. Which way to go now? I asked a pleasant looking young woman (maybe a service-minded secretary with language-skills recently employed at one of the western companies?). She turned my map around a few times, pointed along the busy street, and disappeared into the crowd. It was almost 10 to 9. I started to run. I crossed the street with a herd of other people and continued to jog down the road. There were four lanes on each side, no sidewalks, and the street was lined with ongoing roadwork, forcing me towards the onrushing traffic. Inhaling the exhaust fumes felt like smoking 10 Hungarian cigarettes at once. The next side street was in sight but the name wasn't right. I had been running in the wrong direction.

I turned around, crossed the street again, and headed back to the junction. The camera dangled round my neck. I held my briefcase with my papers, passport, and tape recorder out in front of me, so I could run better. My tie whirled and my jacket fluttered about me. The waving and honking from some of the pedestrians and drivers signaled that I looked very funny, or possibly threatening. More roadwork and another crossroads with a policeman directing the traffic appeared before me. He pointed me in the direction of a side street.

Here it was calm, not a car in sight. Shabby military barracks on both sides. A littered sidewalk where I was greeted by stray mangy dogs and groups of equally stray mangy Russian soldiers (at least that was what I assumed).

Unshaven and wearing dirty wrinkled uniforms, they appeared to lack any morale or belief in the future. They watched me, a foreigner with all the paraphernalia of prosperity, eyeing me from top to toe as if wondering whether they could sell my camera on the black market. I dared not meet the eyes of either dogs or soldiers.

I progressed with hurried steps. Finally I spotted the right street. But what a street it was! Even shabbier than the one with the dogs and soldiers. It was 5 to 9. I ran and saw a sign that said "Electra." It's got to be here! Western Electronics had probably taken over a Hungarian company by that name and moved into their premises. I rushed into the reception, where three Hungarians were standing engaged in conversation. I announced my meeting with Herr Doktor and Western Electronics. "Can you show me to his office, please?" Communication breakdown. I tried again, this time in German. The language confusion become even worse. French? No, mission impossible. Maybe if I write it down? No response. Western Electronics was an unknown concept in this world. They had never heard of such a company here.

Out on the street again. I considered giving up, turning around to hail a cab downtown. Then, suddenly, the street changed. The misery faded, the shabbiness disappeared and fairly normal buildings with normal people and normal cars came in sight. Now what? The street ended. An anonymous building complex, brown, functional style, no numbers, no signs. It can't possibly be here, can it? I ran through one of the gates. Oh yes, Western Electronics, third floor. I was 10 minutes late. I ran up the stairs and was met in the corridor by a secretary. Herr Doktor would receive me soon. I had time for a quick run to the bathroom to wash my hands and face. Herr Doktor came out, speaking German and sounding somewhat irritated. "Wasn't hard to find now, was it? The streetcar runs right by here." I nodded and accepted a cup of coffee.

This story illustrates one of the simplest problems—that of physical access. This problem, trite as it may seem, is known to all organization researchers and does not abate with age or experience. After all, logistics lie at the heart of all organizing, which demands that the right things and the right people be at the right place at the right time. The story shows that getting to an unknown place on time is one of the recurring research nightmares because it symbolizes much more than an organizing failure: namely, the fear of entering an alien landscape. There is a palpable sense of danger, culminating in the story of the meeting with the dogs and Russian soldiers who acquire a terrifying air, becoming monsters from a fairy tale. The author tried to save himself by evoking standard prejudices (women are secretaries and Russian soldiers are potential criminals), a typical reaction that is confirmed in Malinowski's (1967) famous misdemeanors. These fears do not abate even in more familiar surroundings.

MY WORST DAY IN THE FIELD

Here at last, I said to myself as the plane touched down after circling in the air for 20 minutes, due to air traffic congestion. I hurried to get a seat on the first transfer bus to Stockholm City. People muffled up to their noses were everywhere, and everybody was half running. When I got on the bus I tried to think through my schedule for the day and realized that everything was a big question mark, anything could happen.

I had received a phone call at 4 p.m. the day before from BAC Inc. They wondered if I could come up and do six interviews the following day. Since this was probably the best opportunity I would get for a long time, I accepted. I didn't have much background information concerning the company. Nor did I know who I was supposed to meet. I knew nothing about these people's experience or their positions in the company. In other words, I was very badly prepared for the day and it was making me very uneasy.

I recalled the preliminary talks I had had with the company when we discussed the design of my study. I pondered over management's obvious doubts about having the study carried out at all. I remembered their allusions to the scandal caused by a researcher from the Stockholm School of Economics [The researcher wrote a popular book revealing skeletons in the Absolut company closets, while doing dissertation research in the company.] "Here is the agreement you have to sign regarding company secrets, and we want to see the dissertation before it is published." I got the feeling that I was at their mercy, surrounded by their suspicions. Can't they see I am an honest person? Darn, the traffic had come to a halt again. The southbound lanes from Arlanda airport were blocked and wound far down the road, thousands of cars inched their way along in the queues. The thick fumes rose in the chilly morning. The minutes passed quickly but the lane had frozen. Would I get there in time? When I finally arrived at Stockholm City after a bus ride lasting an hour and a half, I managed to hail a cab. The address was unfamiliar to the driver. He had recently moved in from Norrland and was not at all at home in the Stockholm area. I didn't know whether to laugh or cry. He talked and talked, consulted the map several times, but eventually, five minutes after my appointed time, I was in the BAC Inc. main building!

I was introduced to my first interviewee—the production manager. He seemed slightly annoyed by my late arrival despite my excuses. My fingers didn't want to obey me, and the tape recorder resisted me when I took it out. "What do you need the tape recorder for?" "Only for the record, all you say will be kept confidential, no names will be mentioned and it will not be possible to identify anybody." The product manager just kept looking at me, his expression inscrutable.

An uncomfortable sensation was taking hold of me. What was I doing there, why did I put myself in this humiliating situation? Apparently because the joys of discovery are so great and the knowledge area so fascinating that it makes you feel giddy just to think about it.

Back to my "interview victim," as we students often call them. The room was brown and murky and smelled of ingrained tobacco. The product manager never let go of his glowing cigarette. My eyes were getting hazy and the smell was nauseating. His answers to my first questions were stiff and abrupt. I went on to questions that required answers of a descriptive and reflective nature, but he went on answering in the same way as before. I tried to insert questions that might entice him to open up, but he remained indifferent and distant. My questions led nowhere, he didn't understand them and I failed to understand his responses. He was telling me things that seemed devoid of meaning, and kept shuffling papers looking for something he never seemed to be able to find. "This is getting nowhere," I couldn't help thinking. "Isn't time up yet, so I can go on to the next and hopefully more interesting interviewee?" I tried to peek at my watch while forcing myself to be positive, self-assured, and interested in Mr. X's answers.

The next person was a sales manager. He asked about my background and my research and seemed to find the subject intriguing. He described his experiences willingly and happily and responded to all my questions. I got ideas for more questions. The sales manager gave me an exciting tour of the history of the development and the present state of the company. Great! As time flew by, my internal and external memory drives were booted to the brim with valuable information.

We used an extra 5 minutes, as all my questions had not been answered. The sales manager said he could spare some more time but I had to decline since the next person was probably already waiting to see me, according to the schedule. I thanked him profusely and rushed on to the next person . . . who didn't show up. After 10 minutes I located a secretary and discovered that the missing person was on a business trip. I returned to the sales manager, but he had already gone.

The engines of the aircraft started to rumble. On my way home at last! I removed my shoes, leaned my head back and tried to relax. My head was pounding. The day had been hectic, with lunch taken on the run and constant interviewing without a single break. I tried to think through the day, to get behind what had been said. And what hadn't.

Like in the first story, here there was no problem of formal access: It was more than secured, it was forced on the woman researcher. Her difficulty concerned the interaction itself: What does it help that she is "inside" if she cannot reach her respondents?

The next account describes an exploratory visit at Window Makers Incorporated that began at 9 a.m and ended at midnight, including two meals and deep conversations with the owners.

ONE DAY IN THE FIELD: A TRUE STORY

Perhaps my worst day in the field was really my best. Looking back I have some trouble telling exactly what happened that day. Undoubtedly, I was received in a way that I had never experienced before—or since, for that matter. I had never before received such warm treatment from a company as I did at Window Makers. Also, it is very seldom that one gets to experience so many sides of a company in one day. We moved from politeness to emotionality, from economic rationality to philosophy, from professional roles to private ones and from formal organizations to private lives, all within the span of 15 hours. In fact, a single company visit seldom lasts that long or involves so many dimensions. I dare hardly imagine what a Window Makers' apprentice has to go through during the company's 7-week training. A tremendous amount of energy goes into socializing the apprentices into the right kind of thinking and acting. Window making is probably better described as a religion than a trade or a technology. Luckily I was never there long enough to be indoctrinated, although I was probably heading straight for it.

Today I live happily at a distance from the company but I am fascinated each time I read about them and their methods of window restoration in the newspaper. I also reflect upon the fact that this time around I managed to escape from the field without being devoured by it. It could have become dangerous. Perhaps today I would have been one of those walking around in bib-and-brace overalls propagating for recycling and home-mixed paint—who could tell? Research life has its risks, as the field sometimes turns into a battlefield and we have to defend ourselves. But since the field is the best source of knowledge of the world, we'd better pluck up courage and keep going back. The methods are our weapons and with them we can not only defend ourselves but also win laurels.

This story inverts the classic access theme: The difficulty lies not in getting in, but in getting out—physically and mentally. The accounts read like stories from expeditions against dragons hiding in the field waiting to devour the researchers, who come seeking armed with their battery of methods. In the Polish version of the story, the dragon is sent sheepskins stuffed with explosives—a less complimentary picture of the researchers? (On the role of dragons in organization research, read Sievers, 1990.)

The students' stories tell the story of fear: of being devoured, of being lost, of being late, of being annihilated. The disillusioned comment of the second writer ("Why did I put myself . . .") shows that, in the grip of panic, students evoke the holy mission they have been sent into the field to fulfill. But, as on all such missions, doubts creep in. Is it worth it? "It," apparently, is the threat to one's personal identity.

Whose Identity Is Under Scrutiny?

The same theme can be found in many access reports. These are not apprentice fears because they do not abate with experience. They are not "arrival problems" either: I suffer such problems every day in the field, though their character changes daily. Perhaps when these feelings are no longer felt, it will be time to go home: The feeling of estrangement is gone, and with it the main source of insight. The interviewers are interview victims more often than the interviewees. This has certainly been my experience, and there is nothing surprising about it—except perhaps that the theme of threatened identity does not figure more prominently in access stories. The explanation is, perhaps, that when it does, like in Malinowski's (1967) famous diary, it is answered with censoring attempts by the research community. The picture of a researcher's identity threatened by fieldwork violates the image of a mature adult and a competent professional.

As fully socialized adults, or "competent members" as ethnomethodologists put it, we acquire a continuous personal identity. The emphasis put on its stability conceals the fact that such an identity is accompanied by "discontinuous personal diversity" (Davies & Harré, 1991, p. 46). The continuous personal identity is a result of the repetitiveness of the interactions into which people engage. The discontinuous personal identity is the result of the steady element of novelty in the various interactions. Davies and Harré (1991) therefore suggest that instead of speaking of a "self" possessing an essence (or expressing an essence of a person), it is more useful to speak of "positioning," which they understand as "the discursive process whereby selves are located in conversations as observably and subjectively coherent participants in jointly produced story lines" (p. 48). If writing a book can be seen as a conversation, then in writing these words I am engaged in an interactive positioning (trying to position other people as readers) and in a reflexive positioning (trying to position myself as an author). When this book is published and read, then my identity as a writer will be successfully but temporarily established (until the next book, until somebody else questions it, etc.).

Positioning need not be intentional (every act can be interpreted as positioning), but it often is—in interactions with unknown people and in new contexts. Positioning need not lead to establishing a desired identity and it requires continuation—in fact, people continue to construct and reconstruct their identities all through their lives (Gergen, 1991).

What kind of situation produces fieldwork in this respect? Briefly, fieldwork is a situation in which a person leaves his or her own field and more or less established identity to enter another field. Entrance into the new field begins with extensive positioning, especially on the part of the researcher, which is mentioned but not fully shown in the stories. The key to the relative neglect of this theme in organization access reports might be that if identity is considered at all—and it is not a very common topic in discussing field methods—it is usually assumed that the identity of the people in the field is under scrutiny and may be threatened. This is perhaps correct—accounts from the other side are still very few. But there is no doubt that fieldwork is a major threat to the identity of the researcher.

Let me illustrate these threats and their persistent character with notes from my own recent fieldwork. Part of the study consisted of shadowing top city officials in three different units: a finance department, the waterworks, and a public transportation plant. In the course of this study, I met enough different people in different situations to recognize the futility of formulating any "dress for success" advice. Some people were friendly, some were hostile. Some people were attracted by my exoticism, some were repulsed by it. My identity broke into pieces and then mended again, and this was repeated many times. But I have not changed my opinion that the identity threat is the most painful aspect of field organization studies.

FEBRUARY 17, ON THE PLANE TO WARSAW

My heart beats with apprehension, and not because of the flight. What the heck am I doing here? Where am I going? A person of my age should be learning about the world by watching television. But, after all, I am not going to any exotic land but to the country of my birth. What could possibly happen to me?

FEBRUARY 27, ON THE PLANE FROM WARSAW

One question keeps returning in my thoughts finding no answer. Why did they agree to talk to me? Because they couldn't refuse? Why did the people who I was to shadow agree to let me do it? Because they didn't know what they were in for? Take the Finance Director: she was clearly unable to place me, either geographically (where is Lund?) or professionally (university professors in Warsaw apparently don't run around with tape recorders), and yet she agreed without asking for any additional information.

FD is a woman of my own age with a diploma in economics from the agricultural university, a fact which is sometimes taken up by her enemies. It would be interesting to know how she perceives me, a person with a similar diploma from a school across the street. [Warsaw School of Economics and Warsaw School of Agriculture are neighbors across Independence Avenue.] An exercise in symmetrical anthropology would be fascinating indeed.

In her first sentence she told me she was busy as the mayor was waiting for her, in her second she admitted to never having seen my introductory letter, yet in her third she agreed to be shadowed in March. The fourth sentence spoken was mine: I promised to wait for her until she came back from the mayor's office and to interview her then.

Will I ever understand her motives? Do I have to? The interview went very well, although it didn't have much to do with the question-answer scheme. She seemed to be throwing sample anecdotes at me, splash, splash, and after a while, like in an impressionist painting, a figure emerged—a picture of the city finances and of her role in them. The picture was clearer and less fragmented than the ones that emerge from well-structured, analytical answers. Was that due to some mystic communion between two female souls, or to the superiority of narrative knowledge? Funnily enough, my scientific training makes me uneasy when I listen to such image projections. Lists and analyses make me happy—but only until I read them again afterwards.

WARSAW, MARCH 7

9:35. I am truly dragging my feet on my way to the Finance Director's office. I am clearly afraid—but of what? I am fairly sure of FD's sincere intentions. There may perhaps be some minor troubles and difficulties along the way in our 10 days together, but there always are. Nobody wishes me ill. Why be afraid? Because of my total dependence and the necessary passivity, that's why. I am not used to other people controlling my life so literally.

Despite my slow pace I arrive at the office too early. I go down a wrong corridor first, but then arrive at the right door. Will I recognize FD? A woman dressed to go out passes me in the door—God, is it her? No, but she comes next, carrying her fur coat on her arm, ready to meet the deputy mayor before the council session we are all to attend. FD directs me to her deputy, promises to send her car for us, and gives me a draft of the budget to study in the meantime. And a very good thing too, as otherwise I wouldn't have been able to understand much of the session.

12:00. End of the session. I am waiting for FD at the door. FD clearly expects me to go home, but I protest. We return to the office in her car. FD is planning to meet the deputy mayor. I summon up all my courage and ask, "May I go with you?" "No, these matters are not intended for the ears of strangers."

I go into her office, where I claim a place at the conference table which is to be mine in the days to come. She comes in and goes out of the office without explanation. The secretary makes tea for her and she eats her lunch sandwich while looking at her papers.

14:00. FD calls her first deputy: "Take Madam to the cafeteria, I am leaving now."

15:30. I am back in the office when FD returns. "I'm still busy," she says before leaving the office again. She comes back after a while: "Are you still waiting for me?" I smile bravely (or so I think) and promise to be there tomorrow at 8.00. FD protests. This is not how she imagined it. She can't work this way. She thought that I would only be appearing now and then. I feel I am sinking but I try to stay up, and once again to explain to her my way of working. The compromise reached is that I may come the next day at 14.00, after all her important meetings.

WARSAW, MARCH 8

14:00. As I enter the secretary's office, she says: "Madam Finance Director is busy." "I will wait then." "But she has other meetings afterwards." I smile coolly (or so I think) and say, "She told me to come at 14.00." I take my coat off and hang it on a hanger, close to FD's. "At least let her finish this telephone call," says the secretary.

I sit down and prepare to wait. Several people go into FD's office and come out again. I am beginning to feel serious apprehension, when FD finally appears herself: "Are you waiting for me already?" I go into her office and begin to flatter her. "Your budget was accepted in great style! No wonder the telephone never stops ringing. You're the name of the day!" FD smiles thinly but does not send me away. [This comment turns out to represent the peak of my shadowing success in the days to come.] "Perhaps you can tell me about your plans for the next few days so I can try not tire you too much?" The next day she is meeting the city mayor, after which they will both go to meet representatives of a Big Bank—my presence is out of the question. I can come to the office at 14:00. The day after that she's going to Lodz to meet other city finance directors. Too far for me (in her opinion). And the following day again she's visiting one of the districts, but won't be staying long. After that I can hang around, if I insist.

FD seems to be so reconciled to my presence that she promises to help me to arrange an interview with the deputy mayor (which I had failed to do on my own). She calls his secretary and presents my business in great (incorrect) detail, and sends me along there. It is next door. The secretary's office/waiting room is enormous. There are two people sitting there, the secretary and a man whom I assume to be a bodyguard. The secretary talks on the phone while the guard asks me to state my business. I do and he bids me to wait. The secretary stops talking, takes my business card and my introductory letter, and says that the deputy mayor is very busy. Right now he is talking to a journalist. I produce my best smile [I was told afterward by an honest respondent that I smiled far too much for the local custom], and explain that any time during my stay in Warsaw would do.

The deputy's door opens and the journalist comes out. The secretary goes into the office and comes out with the deputy, who shakes my hand without kissing it (what a relief!) and says that he has heard of me but that he's awfully busy. I reply that I haven't counted on meeting him today, but perhaps sometime during the week . . . He and his secretary lean over his completely blank diary and bombard me with his appointments: bus factory all day Wednesday, London on Thursday. . . . [I am not suggesting they were inventing all this. As far as I could establish, nobody used diaries for writing down their appointments. They looked at them to remember days and dates.] I say that I'll be back; he says that he might not be deputy mayor any longer; I say, even better, he would have more time for reflection; he says, not before retirement; I say that would be too long to wait; he says not at all; I say that, after all, we are the same age . . . "Put her in on Wednesday," he says to his secretary. "Which Wednesday? There's a press conference this Wednesday." We decide the date, the day, the hour. [The secretary canceled the appointment later.] . . . He leaves, the telephone rings. The secretary answers: "He just left." She turns to me, sighing: "Poor man, everybody wants him . . . He should change his name to 'Wanted.'" "Jerk," would be my suggestion, but I take several deep breaths and return to the FD's office.

My coat is not on the hanger but lying on a chair. Had I forgotten to hang it up after all? Had somebody taken it down thinking FD's coat was too crowded? The etiquette of fieldwork seems to be beyond my capacity.

FD talks to her deputy about tenders. I ask if they can explain some matters to me that I don't understand. FD agrees—either she is in a good mood or feeling guilty for systematically neglecting me.

15:15. Both leave the office, FD to talk to the deputy mayor—about what? I wish I knew. I'm trying to overhear various conversations in the secretary's office.

15:40. FD comes back. "God! my correspondence is still unanswered, and you're still writing—what?" "All sort of things." I watch her check her correspondence and compare it to my way of doing it. I have a similar letter file, but obviously I'm not using it right.

We leave the office together. I take the opportunity to ask her about the procedure for accepting the budget:

BC: With all due respect, such council sessions are mainly a matter of ritual, aren't they? But are you still apprehensive?

FD: It gets better and better every year, at first I couldn't sleep the night before. But the tension is always there—will they vote to accept it or not?

BC: But can they not accept it?

FD: Well, if they fail to accept it before a certain date, it goes to the Regional Audit Chamber.

BC: Which accepts what the city management—that is you, proposed, doesn't it?

FD: In principle, yes, but how would you feel if somebody questioned your work for the past year? Awful, wouldn't you?

I wish I could report that my relationship with FD improved, but it didn't. It didn't get worse either. She regularly left me for business gossip (of which there was a lot, considering that a major reform was in the offing) and for important business meetings. I spent hours in the secretary's office, overhearing conversations that were both entertaining and informative, talking to FD's deputies, and reading various documents. Because I was not allowed to spend all the working day in the office, I had a lot of time to brood over my inadequacies—as I saw them—as a field researcher. It seemed to me that the main problem was that FD and I were too alike to achieve an easy distance and yet too alien to become close. There was no doubt, however, that we perceived each other as similar, that we were in a symmetrical position. She compared herself to me and I compared myself to her. Similarly, I achieved (temporarily) access to the deputy mayor by pointing out our age symmetry. The issue of similarity also came up in my relations to other people in the field, for example, those I shadowed later. But it was not easy: Similarity, it seems, might both hamper and facilitate access. Such difficulties connected to the doppelgänger position have been discussed in detail by anthropologists.

On the Doppelgänger, or Halfie Research

One of the perennial topics of debate in old anthropology was the ethnological gap that separated the ethnographers from the people who figured in their ethnographies (Lejeune, 1989). Although this gap appeared to be obvious in comparing oral and literate cultures, it seemed to vanish as literacy increased in previously oral societies. The new problem consisted of an ideological gap, that is, the differences between western and non-western vocabularies, between everyday vocabularies and that of intellectual elites, and so on. This gap was filled by writers who undertook to represent the Other—to speak in the Other's voice. Lejeune judges this as just another intellectual illusion and examines interesting examples of workers who have become writers. In doing so, according to Lejeune, these people joined the intellectual elite. If identity is what a person does, then one who writes for a living is an intellectual and not a worker and the question of representation (in its political rather than its statistical sense) remains unsolved.

The problem of representation is quite different in organization studies. Most such studies focus on the managerial group and—leaving aside the complications of such focusing for the moment—this generates problems of its own. Here we have a case of truly symmetrical anthropology (although not in the sense that Latour, 1993, who launched the concept, would have it, i.e., as symmetry between humans and nonhumans, westerners and nonwesterners, society and nature). In principle, this is how it should be, which does not make it easier. The voices of the field reported in organization studies are as literate and eloquent as those of the reporters. They speak in the same (or very nearly the same) language and both have theoretical ambitions. The worry of the conscientious anthropologists— "Do we silence them by speaking for them?"—becomes "How can we be heard?" There are at least three groups in competition with one another: managers, researchers, and professional consultants. If researchers represent managers, to whom do they represent them? If the researcher's role is to give the managers feedback, how can she or he convince managers that the picture presented will be of use to them? Can researchers say anything the managers do not already know?

The accounts above do refer to such difficulties, but the clearest illustration of the problem I have found comes from Gideon Kunda's (1992) corporate ethnography. One of the main characters in Kunda's story is a woman employed by the company who taught "organization culture" courses and who had just completed a PhD dissertation in anthropology on this very subject. Who was studying whom and for what purpose? If Kunda's dissertation work had been done earlier, she would have included him in her account from the field. Is so-called fieldwork then nothing but a narcissistic exercise? Could I write a diary instead of interrupting FD's working hours?

I see this entanglement as an opportunity rather than a problem. To begin with, this problematic symmetry successfully prevents researchers from objectifying the people they study. A feminist sociologist friend of mine, who made several studies of unemployed women, was startled by her experiences in a new project involving top female politicians and managers. "I always thought I had very good contact with the women in the field," she said to me. "I still think so, but after I'd been sent packing several times, I began to see how much of that contact depended on the implicit assumption that the unemployed women had to cooperate with me as it was all 'for their good.' " This change of perspective has been noticed by many anthropologists who have studied industrialized countries. Schwartzman (1993), quoting anthropologist Laura Nader (1974), speaks of "studying up" as opposed to "studying down" (pp. 27-46). Schrijvers

(1991), alluding to Nader's notions, speaks of "studying sideways," claiming that it presents the best conditions for a dialogical relationship with the field. I agree: The unsentimental idea of a relationship to the study object that is a subject, that is, that speaks back, seems to have best premises in sideways studies, of which organization studies are perhaps the most clear example.

Another advantage lies in the very uneasiness I reported above as a source of knowledge of one's own and of one's doppelgänger role and position in the organizational world. The mutual proximity is such that there is no danger of fascination with the exotic; the distance persists and begs to be explored.

A third advantage is that this kind of field research, which compels intensive positioning comparable to that required by a job change or some similar rupture in day-to-day life, makes the researchers aware of the *positionality* of their own and other people's views and actions. This last concept I borrow from Lila Abu-Lughod's (1991) discussion of *halfie research,* that is, anthropological research done by "people whose national or cultural identity is mixed by virtue of migration, over-seas education or parentage" (p. 138). The analogy is quite obvious. There, as here, the anthropologist's assumption of a fundamental distinction between the self and the Other is called in question. This distinction in anthropology, Abu-Lughod claims, was always hierarchical, in the sense that the (western) self is superior to the (nonwestern) Other. What happens when, as in the cases discussed here, the Other is more powerful than the self?

One effect, it seems to me, is a somewhat paradoxical emergence of more sensitive, richer (and humbler) studies. This might be seen as leading to further reduction of the reading audience, which was never too large. After all, stories written by the powerful have an attraction on their own, as Foucault has made us aware, and a usual strategy recommended by method books is to create an impression of a powerful author. A strategy that involves resigning power might thus seem puzzling in such terms, and choosing a narrative approach to organization studies implies such a strategy in contrast to the "we-know-better" paradigmatic approach.

But power alone does not decide the size of the audience. There is always beauty and use (an ardent pragmatist may even count beauty as a kind of use). There is a hope that humble stories might conquer the audience by their aesthetic value. Abu-Lughod (1991) ends on a similar note when she advocates writing "ethnographies of the particular" (p. 149) as opposed to generalized accounts. She notes that although interpretative approaches began with criticizing positivist social science for its ignorance of the centrality of meaning to human experience, they ended up substituting "generalizations about meanings for generalizations about behavior" (p. 150).

My vision of ergonographies, that is, ethnographies of work organizations (see Chapter 5, "Doing the Reading and Doing the Writing: From the Field to the Text"), is just an example of ethnographies of the particular. This does not mean losing the global perspective or anything similar. The global perspective can be reached only by studying how different locals are connected to one another. Or, to put it bluntly, there is no micro- and macroworld influencing one another. The results of this widespread misapprehension are sometimes tragic and sometimes comic. It appears that a coffee pause in Brussels happens on an international level, one in Stockholm is national, and in Gothenburg it is local. An event that takes place in headquarters is global, of course, whereas the same event in a local plant is, by definition, local.

An alternative outlook is that there are only different perspectives, and a macroperspective is a view that encompasses many microevents at once. Not everybody is permitted to make use of the macroperspective, however, because it has obvious power implications. It is certainly not by accident that the rulers favor macroresearchers and that researchers taking a macroperspective think themselves indispensable to rulers. To be able to control at a distance, one must objectify people first (Latour, 1992). For this reason, microstudies are more often than not on the side of the underdogs, be they managers or workers, and on the side of the rebellion. By showing how macropictures are drawn, microstudies problematize the taken for granted.

Perhaps it is this meddling with the taken for granted that makes the threats toward personal and professional identity unavoidable. The psychological discomfort of estrangement seems to be a necessary price of learning. The bonus lies in extra knowledge that researchers may gain about themselves. The main compensation is a problematized picture of organizational reality. Such a picture carries a possibility of liberation for those who suffer from the reality they were led to construct and a promise of a nontrivial story for the researcher.

NOTE

1. The stories are used here by the authors' permission.

Familienspaziergang (Paul Klee, 1930)

4 SCIENCE AS CONVERSATION
A Story of Referencing and Referencing as Story Telling

Texts on method have traditionally focused on the process of conducting the study, assuming that once discovered, truth will write itself. The emphasis has shifted to the processes of writing and reading research reports, as my own attempt illustrates. Not much attention has been paid to the practices of quoting and referencing in organization studies assumed to be technical details.[1] A reflection over our current referencing practices might prove interesting, not least from the narrative perspective. What do these practices say and what do they do? What kind of an image of science is behind these practices?

Science is commonly but implicitly seen as an accumulating body of knowledge covered by the laws protecting private property. An author has the right to borrow any piece on the condition of paying royalties—literally or symbolically: thus, the obligation of giving a source of ideas, thoughts, and sentences. A contrasting image of science is that civilization, science, and education constitute a conversation that goes on for five millennia:

> As civilized human beings, we are the inheritors neither of an inquiry about ourselves and the world, nor of an accumulating body of information, but of a conversation begun in the primeval forest and extended and made more articulate in the course of centuries. (Oakeshott, 1959/1991, p. 490)

Oakeshott (1959/1991) concludes that conversation's rules and mores change over the years. Referencing can be seen as a special mode of conversation with rules of its own. These, in turn, can be derived from the modern institution of copyrights. I will therefore venture on a brief historical excursion into the field of copyrights, from which the practices of referencing have arisen.

A Short History of Referencing

Throughout this narrative, I will use the thesis formulated by Boyle (1992) as a supporting thesis: that the copyright laws draw their legitimacy from 19th-century liberalism, within which two traditions are especially relevant. One is concerned with the image of property, society, and privacy in a liberal state. Another is the romantic image of an author who produces an original idea (out of nothing, as it were) that is clearly distinguishable from a mere "expression." Boyle argues, and I follow him in this argument, that these traditions are both amazingly well and alive and yet increasingly out of date in our "information society."

THE DIFFUSED AUTHORSHIP IN PREMODERNITY AND ITS END

Greek and Roman historians considered it their duty to report what people said, and it was not unusual that they mentioned, after say 600 pages of stories, that they themselves did not believe a word. It was the reader's task to decide what to believe. Veyne (1988) claims that, for instance, Herodotus was highly skeptical toward the history presented by himself. But evaluation of the sources or indeed of the authenticity of the stories was beyond the point. Writers were collectors of oral stories that constituted the main source of knowledge and the means of transmitting tradition. They were valued and admired, but their role was that of doing a service to the community; indeed, Veyne compares these writers to contemporary journalists. If they did not collect contemporary stories, they were looking for ancient knowledge, like Greek philosophers, who mostly looked toward the Orient for the font of knowledge but rarely reached for texts written in languages other than Greek (Eco, 1990). In high antiquity, people wanted their books to be complete and thus made all the necessary changes and additions to keep them updated. This tradition survived even in high modernity: Today one can find in India contemporary versions of the Upanishad mentioning the invention of electricity and other modern events (Veyne, 1988). In those times, texts were not copied but made anew by combining them with other texts. Originality was of no value.

The Middle Ages brought in the copyists but did not change the view on originality. Medieval church writers tended to disapprove of originality and valued the scribe and the copyist above the author. Only God had the monopoly on truth, and humans were stenographers for divinities. Church writers perceived their own mission as one of finding valuable old books that could then be copied for the use of future generations (Boyle, 1992). This can be seen as a pragmatic solution in a situation where there was no way of establishing the exact provenience of a given manuscript.

Veyne (1988) observes that, for example, Thomas Aquinas did not refer to Aristotle in his reinterpretations of the Greek's thoughts. Aquinas took sole responsibility for his text, which he takes as a testimony to truth and which does not have an author. *Authenticus,* says Eco (1990), meant to Aquinas and his contemporaries not "original" but "true." This usage was common for a long time. Veyne tells the story of a French historian, Etienne-Pasquier, who in 1560 sent the manuscript of his book to his friends for comments:

> Their most frequent reproach concerned Pasquier's habit of giving too many references to the sources he cited. This procedure, they told him, cast a "scholastic pall" on the book and was unbecoming in a work of history. Was it truly necessary each time to confirm his "words by some ancient author"? If it was a matter of lending his account authority and credibility, time alone will see to that. (p. 6)

Pasquier was ahead of his time: Very soon after, conventions of writing science began to change. References started to appear in juridical texts at the end of the 17th century in what Veyne (1988) calls "works of controversy" (p. 11). Veyne sees it as an indication that references have litigious origin, where the authors write to their own colleagues, prone to doubt their statements. "Proofs were flaunted about before they were shared with the other members of the 'scientific community' " (p. 11). The emergence of such a community had in turn to do with the rise of university and academic profession. Montaigne and Montesquieu, for example, were men of riches who lived leisurely off their estates and wrote to whomever wanted to read them. No academic contestant could question their authority because it did not come from academia (Grayson, 1995).

Not without significance was the accompanying development of proof procedures, which in our times have became so sophisticated with technologies of examinations and such other wonders that forgery and plagiarism have had to become highly technological to keep pace (Eco, 1990). Although forgery and plagiarism thrive mainly in art, there are great many stories of forgeries, plagiarisms, and falsifications in academia.

It has taken a myriad of litigation and the development of many supporting institutions for copyright to develop (the central part of which was the invention of print and other mass replication techniques), but the issue of academic quarrels is always instructive. I will mention just two that, because of their spectacular character, illustrate how the new ways of dealing with litigation took shape.

One of them is the theme of Robert Merton's (1965/1985) book, *On the Shoulders of Giants.* In *OTSOG,* as he calls it lovingly and with some irony toward the U.S. way of abbreviating everything, Merton intends to show that so-called epochal discoveries (he picks Newton as the main example) were in fact either reformulations of already existing ideas and/or something that was already in the social air, so to speak, and it is mostly by chance that one person is seen as the author and not another (Isaac Newton's contestant was Robert Hooke). In fact, it is only centuries later that one name is ascribed to an idea: At the time of "discovery," the contenders fight bitterly for copyrights and, as in the case of Popov and Marconi, the fight may remain undecided.

Western readers might not know that the Soviet Union had its own contender to the invention of the radio, Aleksandr Popov. He built his first primitive radio receiver, a lightning detector, in 1896 without the knowledge of the contemporary work of the Italian inventor Guglielmo Marconi, who patented his invention in England in June the same year. As the *Britannica* from 1990 gently puts it, "The genuineness and the value of Popov's successful experiments are not seriously doubted, but Marconi's priority is usually conceded outside the Soviet Union" (p. 607). It was Marconi, not Popov, who received the Nobel Prize for Physics in 1909. What is rewarded then is priority, not the idea. Merton's thesis is that all ideas are around all the time and that the ascription of authorship is a result of chance and clever politics.

THE MODERN INSTITUTION OF COPYRIGHTS

In modern times, academia has openly become an agonist if not straightforward antagonist field. Parties fight: for priority, for patents, for fame, and for positions. The means of adjudication are needed and developed. But it is impossible to patent an idea if it does not acquire a physical form, and this is usually in the form of a document. *Copyright* is the central institution in this respect. The Statute of Anne passed in England in 1710 is considered a turning point in the history of copyright law in the sense that it took the rights from the local government and turned them toward authors and publishers, setting an example for other countries to follow. Before that, or at least before 1625, the term *plagiarism* did not exist in English (Boyle, 1992).

In Germany, several factors were at work in the 17th century. On the one hand, the reading public grew enormously; on the other, there were tales spreading (true or not) about sad fates of popular authors dying of starvation and misery. Enhanced by the emergence of the romantic notion of the author, writers (poets, novelists, and philosophers) demanded money and the right to their products.

Not everybody thought it was a good idea—then as now. Some authors pointed out that the notion of intellectual property is an oxymoron. You might have a monopoly on an idea if you keep it to yourself, but how can you maintain it after publication? Then it belongs to everybody! The main tenet of the romantic notion of authorship was that it was based on inspiration, not on craftsmanship. Eighteenth-century theorists, says Woodmansee (1984), minimized the element of craftsmanship in favor of the element of inspiration, which came to be understood in terms of original genius. Consequently, inspired work was made the product and the property of the writer. Such understanding of written work rejects the idea of a "proper method" or a "workshop" in which one could be an apprentice, literally or metaphorically. The author was he (yes, yes) who changed the genre, who revolutionized the form.

It was the German philosopher Fichte who, according to Boyle (1992), found a satisfactory answer to the question as to how an author can maintain the right to an idea that has been published ("made public"):

> Fichte disaggregated the concept of property in books. The buyer gets the physical thing and the ideas contained in it. *Precisely because the originality of the spirit was converted into an originality of form* the author retains the right to the form in which those ideas were expressed. (p. 1466)

The same idea is behind copyright in design and, says Boyle, it permeates U.S. law in its entirety.

Market economy and mass production led to the commodification and commercialization of culture, including literature and science. So far almost everybody agrees: The point of contention is whether this development should be lamented or celebrated. Critical theorists, following the lead of the Frankfurt School, see in the copyright tradition not so much romanticization as commercialization of thought. In his gloomy but interesting book *The Decline of Discourse,* Agger (1990) compares academic writing to the real estate business: Both are a matter of clever acquisitions and swift speculations. In this business, citations have the main function of supporting the self-replication of the academic system, and copyrights concern not so much ideas as property rights to a given place, or rather space, in the system. "After all, academics write *for themselves,* and for others like them. They write not to be read but to command space, the basis of value in the academic world" (p. 136).

To be read, a writer must quote others; to be able to continue to write, a writer must be quoted by others—so turn the mills of normal science. The idea of references as property was hinted at by many other authors, for example, Kaplan (1965) and Ravetz (1971). Kaplan observes that citation practices solve the dilemma of knowledge as common property and individual property based on priority. Scientists may not keep their products, but they are rewarded for production by points earned on early delivery.

This recurring idea is refused by Gilbert (1977), who points out the shortcomings of the property rights metaphor. There are several things to be said in its defense, though. To begin with, to call references "property rights" is not really to speak metaphorically, as the previous discussion suggests: This is what they are, historically speaking. But even if we argue that historical origins are less important than contemporary usage and therefore it is but a metaphor, Gilbert attacks the representative aspect of the metaphor as weak, ignoring its expressive potential, that is, what truly makes a metaphor effective (Eco, 1979/1983). Gilbert attacks the property rights perspective on referencing to claim that references are really meant as a means of persuasion, not as prosperity indexes. There is no reason to disagree that references are used as a means of persuasion, but so are many other objects of property.

Anyway, the modern institution of copyrights permits various uses of quotations and references—as indexes of prosperity, as means of persuasion, as historical landmarks (which is a use I am propagating here). It has been said about Walter Benjamin, the patron of the postmodernists, that his use of quotes resembled a "surrealistic montage":

Quotations are at the very center of every work of Benjamin's. This very fact distinguishes his writings from scholarly works of all kinds in which it is the function of quotations to verify and document opinions, wherefore they can safely be relegated to the Notes. . . .The main work [in his case] consisted in tearing fragments out of their context and arranging them afresh in such a way that they illustrated one another and were able to prove their *raison d'être* in a free-floating state . . . (Arendt, 1969, p.47)

Observe that even such use of quotations requires and assumes individual copyright—if the fragments could not be clearly ascribed, the effect would be lost—but they obviously go against the grain of the copyright idea as a means of patenting a thought. The same can be said about practices described by Agger and Kaplan. Has the idea of copyright outlived itself?

THE UNCERTAIN FATE OF COPYRIGHTS IN INFORMATION SOCIETY

This short history of the institution of copyright shows how contemporary institutions are sedimented with practices, values, and beliefs that are long forgotten and yet somehow live under the surface of our consciousness. It is hard to imagine a more drastic contrast than that between the notion of the romantic authorship and writing as practiced in many organization studies journals. There is no question that inspiration and originality are all but forbidden, correct method is all that counts, and as to pecuniary rewards and the applause from the enchanted public, let us say that they are rather indirect. Yet we insist on the value of intellectual property perhaps more than ever.

Not that this is a predicament limited to organization studies: On the contrary, these may suffer less from what is more acute in other fields, from the clear unfeasibility of copyrights in information society. Boyle (1992) lists the most obvious examples of questions raised by the circumstances in which we live now:

What is the distinction between an idea and an expression? Are the page numbers in the West Law Reports or the alphabetical compilations of names in a telephone directory actually copyrightable? What are the criteria for deciding such cases: The originality of the work? The amount of labor that has gone into it? The potential loss to the original compiler or potential profit to the copying party, or to the society? Can anyone own "facts"? Does a computer program such as *Windows* infringe the copyright of the Apple operating system if it has a similar "look" or "feel," regardless of whether look or feel is produced by lines of a computer code that in no way resembles the original work? (p. 1427)

These are only the most obvious examples of copyright problems that mount daily. When all organization studies journals are accessible on Netscape, the possibilities for plagiarism and for checks against it will multiply incredibly. What is going to happen next?

Boyle (1992) spins three possible scenarios, two gloomy, one optimistic. In one version, copyrights will soon be the basis for the punishment of the authors, not for rewards. We may be heading toward an "information pollution" where not only will we be forced to abandon the Enlightenment's dream of the more information, the better, but we will punish people who produce it and pollute the environment. More conventional is the prediction of an emergence of an "information class"—people who benefit from the manipulation of information at the expense of the sources. We see the beginning of this problem in the postcolonial disputes, but also on a small scale in our own field, in which we present ourselves as the truth holders at the expense of organizational actors. So far they win, but who knows what the future holds. In a similar vein, one can point out well-known but never documented cases where "café philosophers" part freely with their ideas, which then get copyrighted by people with the inclination to write rather than to talk.

Against all these sad versions is one optimistic version. Information society will witness more democratic distribution of this good. What is needed is the debunking of romantic authorship (attempted by Barthes, 1979, and Foucault, 1979, until now without much success) and its replacement with a more pragmatic version of creation as bricolage, and of quote as a collage, as legitimate use of accessible cultural elements.

Referencing as Ritual or as Story Telling?

One must ask about the consequences of understanding science as conversation and the knowledge of the history of referencing for the present practices of referencing. One consequence, which I endorse here, is that references can tell a story of their own. After all, the date of the original publication indicates when the conversation first took place, although the date of publication quoted is a help and a courtesy to the contemporary reader. The time of the original conversation is important not because of some historical pedantry, but because it indicates its intended participants.

An interesting example is Warren, Rose, and Bergunder's (1974) *The Structure of Urban Reform,* which epitomizes organization studies from an institutionalist perspective but was published when the old institutionalism seemed to be buried for good and the new institutionalism (usually dated since Meyer & Rowan, 1977) had not yet emerged. The most quoted author is Eric Trist ("sociotechnical systems"), on the surface the least likely conversation partner for institutionalists. But in those days, sociotechnical systems were a major topic of conversation and it would be impolite, not to say unpolitical, not to mention them. Such and other stories can be read (or speculated about) from references, although not all references are keen on telling stories.

REFERENCING THAT KILLS THE STORY

Because all narratives are grounded in chronology, the sure way of killing a potential story is ahistorical referencing, which is accomplished both by alphabetical ordering and by quoting the last edition only.[2] My favorite example is "Weber, 1964," from which it is easy to deduce that all Weber knew about organizations he learned from March and Simon (1958). "Weber, 1964" carries, in fact, yet another story: Postwar German sociologists received Weber mostly in the guise of his retranslations from Parsons, Bendix, and other structural functionalists. Attempts are now being made in Germany to recover Weber from the hands of structuralists (see Hennis, 1996).

Of course, it is not as easy as it may sound. Decisions must be made. If we quote Weber as "1947," which is when Talcott Parsons translated his book into English, we are correct insofar that we have never seen the original, and for all we know, Parsons might have invented it. But *Wirtschaft und Gesellschaft* was published in 1922. These are more technical decisions that can be made individually depending on the issue in question, however. I am speaking now about more basic issues. It may seem but a common courtesy to remember who said what first, but one must not dismiss the possibility that March and Simon in 1958 were answering some question posed by Weber in English in 1947 and in German in 1922.

Another common habit is to pack into one set of parentheses the names of people who, if alive, would not speak to each other and if dead would avoid the same cemetery. "Marx and March" is an easy example because both authors have something to say about power, but they do not speak the same language and most likely are not even speaking about the same phenomenon. After all, words are but loosely coupled to their social referents. Sometimes those authors invest their lives in opposing each other's views that they find unacceptable, and then they are put into one bracket with disregard for beliefs, standpoints, and ideologies. The idea of accumulating knowledge does not agree very well with the idea of persistence of opposing ideas.

One practice that threatens referencing as story telling is what could be called shopping-list referencing (Brown, 1977; Carlsson, 1980; Czarniawska-Joerges, 1975,1976,1978,1984,1991; Debussy, 1950; Einstein, 1924; Forssell, 1992). Obviously, a list of names is not a text: It is by definition a list, that is, a set of discrete elements in which connections between elements remain unexplored. The value of such lists is informative, not argumentative or narrative. But then why put such a list in the middle of an argument or a narrative? If the items thus listed have any importance for the argument, they will show up in the appropriate place. If they do not have any relevance for the argument, why are they there at all?

Readers might suspect that referencing is meant to replace the argument: "Highlighting contradictions (Brown & Smith, 1985) we arrive at a stock-of-knowledge (Schutz, 1973) in order to be able to explore *la différance* proper (Derrida, 1966/1978)." Unfortunately, this quote is almost genuine (I stylized it somewhat to avoid recognition). The sentence sounds positively Rosicrucian, but the problems involved are more than just laughable. What is funny is that the sentence does not *say* anything, it only *does* something (Silverman & Torode, 1980): it shows the author's familiarity with jargon. It also employs a style that to my aesthetic is clumsy but to the author's may not be: referencing the clauses, not full sentences.

But "stock of knowledge" and "*différance*" are special problems. Certain authors have copyrights on certain vocabularies: "stock of knowledge at hand" belongs to Alfred Schütz (1953/1973), "standpoint" to Dorothy Smith (1989), "*différance*" to Jacques Derrida (1966/1978). Thus, it is perhaps unnecessary to write an exegesis of Schütz every time one says "purpose at hand" or "stock of knowledge," but a simple "Schütz, 1953/1973" might not suffice for a reader who is not familiar with Schütz's work. There are no ready solutions to this problem: As in the course of a field study, each step requires a decision and often hides an ethical problem. References, connections to other texts, often lead to other people as well.

Another problem, felt acutely by some readers, is counterargument referencing. In referencing a critical argument, it is often uncertain whether the author quoted is guilty of what is criticized or criticized it first (Smith, 1972). Similarly, in the case of "stock of knowledge, Schutz 1973," we do not know (if we don't know the expression already) whether Schutz was a guy who had a stock of knowledge or the guy who invented the expression. Please also take note that thanks to the advancements in computer technology, Alfred Schütz can posthumously enjoy his name in its correct version, that is, "Schütz," not "Schutz."

Counterreferencing is actually only a variation on referencing in place of the argument. If an argument is fully developed, readers will know whether the sentence above means that, as Smith (1972) rightly pointed out, it is difficult to guess whether the authors quote an example or the source or that this tendency is best if unfortunately illustrated by writings of Smith (1972). Observe that it is difficult to put—sensibly—two different references into one sentence, not to mention five.

REFERENCING THAT TELLS A STORY

Referencing that aspires to tell a story must be integrated into an argument. There are two main ways of integrating a text written by somebody else into one's own text. One is an *exegetic* way of referencing. In this mode, the other author's text stands in focus: as a model, as an object of criticism, or as material for a proper exegesis. The main thing then is to *represent* the author as faithfully as possible (if I could recall who said that in order to criticize you must first understand, I would have referenced it), and then take a stance: apologetic, critical, a step beyond. Unfortunately, the exegetic tradition is not very well developed in my discipline; Anthony Giddens is the closest example of an author frequently given to exegeses I can think of.

Another, much more common, way of referencing is *inspirational,* which is close to Michel de Certeau's (1984) idea of reading as poaching. I like the concept of structuration and I give the copyrights their due (Giddens, 1981), but I use it for my purposes, in the way I see fit.

Borrowing some terminology from Barthes (1979) and Foucault (1979), I could say that in the first case I am referencing the author and not the work; in the second I am making use of a text whose writer has copyrights to it and is important only in that sense. In the first case, I pay tribute to Giddens; in the second, I prevent him from suing me, thus protecting myself from the accusation of plagiarism.

One interesting complication connected with referencing stems from the fact that it is conventionally assumed that the more references the better. This leads to at least two curious practices. One is referencing clichés: Life is a search for meaning, but this has been said many times before, for example, Victor Frankl (1973), so—unless one wishes to present Frankl's fascinating philosophy—there should hardly be a point in referencing this statement. A similar matter arises in connection with notions and statements that become classic (after all, this is what clichés are). Snow's two cultures and Derrida's *différance* can go unreferenced, sometimes even by a name. But a notion of a classic is relative: Ask your students who Gerard Phillippe was. You don't know yourself? Then you must be under 35. Look in reference books on French films.

The other peculiar practice produced by considering referencing as a virtue per se is quoting sources that the author considers bad on the assumption that all relevant literature must be referred to. Because there are too many sources now to do any thorough critique of all of them, scientific writers save themselves by quoting the relevant authors in a long shopping list. The loser is the reader, who has to go through piles of scientific products only to discard some.

If references tell a story of their own, it makes sense to turn to historians and literary critics for models. In these disciplines, texts are seen as events, not only as indexes of legal rights and records of priority. Citing Merton's *OTSOG* as "1965/1985" is not analogous with establishing when cold fusion was first achieved. It tells us an interesting fact that a book written in 1965 became relevant in 1985; from that we can speculate that the 1960s and the 1980s had more in common than the 1970s. It may be an incorrect speculation, but it is worth investigating. And so it goes, especially for exegetic approaches. First names make authors human and give women authors their due. I am aware that some women authors are afraid that the revelation of their gender will lead to a discriminatory reading. Correct as this suspicion might be, the practice of hiding the gender only perpetuates the status quo. Many more women created organization studies as we know them than is commonly believed. Publishers sometimes prohibit the use of first names in the text, which dehumanizes the authors. True, they are but fictitious model authors created by readers, but even a model author has a right to a first name.

Using last names only is dictated also by economy of space. I try to indicate in this way the difference between the exegetic and the inspirational mode. I take from Brown (1977) his symbolic realism for my private uses, a very different case from the one when I present Richard H. Brown (1977, 1980, 1987, 1989) as a precursor of narrative approaches to organization studies.

Even bibliographies tell stories and thus require serious referencing: first name, initial, last name, date of first publication, date of the edition quoted, publisher, place, pages. There are many instrumental reasons for this, as any publisher will tell, but also at least one symbolic reason. Exact references confirm that the text belongs to a genre: Social science is written in a realist convention. Although these are no experimentally stated facts, the references fulfill the same function: They promise that a text can be checked against reality. Referencing might be but a convention resulting from the modern institution of copyrights, but discovering that the year of publication is wrong in some items can put at risk the credibility of the whole enterprise. When Jean d'Ormesson fakes all references in his pseudoscientific historical novel, I am delighted; when an author of a purportedly scientific article fakes the sources to pull my leg, I am still delighted; when somebody demanding serious attention does not get his or her references right, I am disenchanted. And right now, while the readers turn bloodthirstily toward my reference list, I feel apprehensive . . .

As a writer of organization studies, I fight against memory lapses, vanishing traces, and tricky computers to keep my references straight. As a reader of organization studies, I hope to find in references a meta-story of the topic, a trace of conversations between texts that occurred in a concrete time and place. Past conversations, like personal memories, can be reweaved into present conversations and thus acquire a meaning beyond the faithful remembrance of things past.

NOTES

1. An earlier and different version of this chapter was published in Swedish (Rombach, 1994).

2. Some references in this chapter are made up. I hope that the readers will be able to decide for themselves which are which.

Der Weg von Unklaich nach China (Paul Klee, 1920)

5 DOING THE READING AND DOING THE WRITING
From the Field to the Text

The two previous chapters were intended to be self-exemplifying. I used narrative devices—collecting and interpreting stories—on the material from the field of organizational research. This chapter is dedicated to a reflection on what a narrative approach consists of—in the light of those examples—and what its possible uses might consist of.

Let me begin with a trite but important observation that when attempts to collect material from the field have been successful, the researcher is rewarded with a pile of texts. Some are written in numbers, some in words; some are written by the researcher (e.g., interview records and field notes) and some are written by other people (e.g., documents and press clippings). This does not matter all that much; the task is to interpret the information and come up with a new text that will bear this interpretation.

Reading the Field

There is a host of interesting options for those who need to read texts from the field. There are excellent instructions on how to proceed (e.g., Feldman, 1995, on ethnomethodology, semiotic analysis, dramaturgical analysis, and deconstruction; Martin, 1990, on deconstruction; Riessman, 1993, on narrative analysis; Silverman, 1993, on conversation analysis; Silverman & Torode, 1980, on interruption). I would like to comment briefly only on the difference between conversation analysis and discourse analysis, which tends to baffle my students. The students are quite justified in their puzzlement, however, because there is one established tradition (Ricoeur, 1981) that treats these terms as synonyms and another one that

Conversation Analysis	Discourse Analysis
Conversation, from *conversare* (to live, to keep company with; obsolete: conduct, behavior): oral exchange of sentiments, observations, opinions, or ideas.	Discourse, from *discurrere* (to run about): formal and orderly, usually extended expression of thought on a subject.
Ethnomethodology: Actors (talkers) are visible and central.	Discourse analysis: (Foucault, Barthes) Discourse is impersonal; no actors (talkers) are visible or needed.

includes conversations into discourse analysis (Potter & Wetherell, 1987). Keeping the difference might have its pragmatic uses, as I will try to show. Such differences can be justified by the etymology of the two words (*Webster's New Collegiate Dictionary,* 1981) and the two traditions behind their use, as shown above.

Thus, conversation analysis treats talk as action, whereas discourse analysis treats talk as talk. Conversation analysis captures and analyzes a concrete speech situation located in a point in time and space. Discourse analysis addresses many conversations that take place over time in different locations and yet that seem to be connected. Although conversation analysis uses transcripts or videotapes of a concrete interaction, discourse analysis collects various types of inscriptions of "conversations" that perhaps were never enacted in the ordinary meaning of the word. From the narrative perspective, the two analyses are complementary. The institutionalized discourse serves as a repertoire for actual conversations; these in turn reproduce and change the discourse. A research report is a conversation within the social science discourse: written exchange of sentiments, observations, opinions, and ideas. The exchange is a forced one because it has been arranged by the writer of the report: Texts authored by people who never speak to one another are forced to converse in yet another text.

Saying this, however, I am already moving from reading to writing; indeed, I do not think that these two can be separated for long. Private reading exists, but it never reaches a larger audience, which is only aware of a reading that has been made public—by inscription, by writing.

A field research report is therefore a compilation of texts authored by practitioners, theoreticians, and the author herself or himself. The analogy that comes to mind is that of a literary collage (after all, the computer command "paste"), although, in deference to Walter Benjamin, it is often called a literary *montage* (e.g., Cappetti, 1995; Pred, 1995). A collage also makes visible this particular mixture of reproduction and production that every reading and writing necessarily entails.

Two aspects need to be brought to the fore in relation to the collage analogy. Although field reports always were collages, work and skill were put into softening the edges, in erasing the different authorships, in achieving the illusion of one voice telling one story. Calling the research report a collage is an encouragement to make it clearly polyphonic, where the authorship of different pieces is distinctly attributed.

This does not mean that the role of the reader/writer should be effaced. Collage is the work of an author, and the pieces are used to acquire a new meaning by being recontextualized. Polyphony is actually nothing else than a *variegated speech,* as Bakhtin (1928/1985) says, a writer's trick that enriches the text but also, more important, reminds readers that the world is full of different voices, differing vocabularies, and disparate dialects, that there cannot be one story of the world.

Even gluing disparate pieces together amounts to an act of reading. It is therefore not out of place to recall the hermeneutic triad, a way of representing interpretive procedures of which many variations exist. I shall refer to Hernadi (1987), who classifies interpretation into three stages: explication, explanation, and exploration. *Explication* is reproductive translation in which the interpreter chooses to stand *under* the text, in Frye's (1973) term, aiming at understanding it. *Explanation* is an employment of an inferential detection to analyze it, in which the reader stands *over* the text. This can be done in many ways, depending on the preference of the reader. The conventional scientific analysis sees this stage as an explanation of the seepage from reality into the text.

Social scientists have a professional duty to proceed to the third stage, *exploration,* in which readers stand *in for* the author, thus constructing a new text, although with an original one as a starting point. This might mean constructing a text from scratch (in opposition to the one already existing), a reconstruction, or a deconstruction of the one that exists.

Returning to the short narrative used in the beginning of this book, the interpretation might go through all three stages as follows: "This is a story of a woman who failed to receive a promotion due to her. The reason for it is the persistent discrimination of women in workplaces. In her place, I would go to the court and make my case known to people in my professional network."

Such readings can be many and varied, but they can also happen at another level. Imagine a reader who goes through the three stages but in the following way: "The original text is very short on detail, thus creating an ambiguity that permits many interpretations. This is typical for texts where the authors expect the readers to project their own experience into the text. Such a textual strategy might misfire, however, because the authors are known to be professional women and therefore can be identified with the woman in the text."

The first reading is close to the text and represents an attitude that Eco (1992) calls that of a naive (semantic) reader. Such readers assume that the text carries a message and tries to render this message by direct quote, a repetition, or by retelling it; look at the seepage from reality (Is it true? How could it have happened?); and identify with the author or the character in the stage of exploration. A semiotic (critical) reader looks in the first place for a seepage from other texts:

> The former uses the work as semantic machinery and is the victim of the strategies of the author who would lead him a little by little along the series of provisions of expectations. The latter evaluates the work as an aesthetic product and enjoys the strategies implemented in order to produce a Model Reader of the first level [i.e., a semantic reader]. (Eco, 1990, p. 92)

An aspiring semiotic reader often asks for help (semantic readers usually have confidence in their "natural" attitude). What should one look for? What do the clues look like? How are connections established between one text and all the others? Such questions are frequent, and there are some attempts to answer them: That is the formalized analytical technique. But there are no interpretation rules. As Ricoeur (1981) says, "There are no rules for making good guesses. But there are methods for validating guesses" (p. 211). The operation of abduction as described by Peirce and practiced by Sherlock Holmes (Eco & Sebeok, 1983) is central in reading texts. Both semantic and semiotic readings of the story of a woman who missed a promotion entail hypotheses: "There are many such cases in organizations," and "The authors wanted to push the readers into a projection mode." In the first case, the readers must check the statistics on gender discrimination; in the second, they must read the research paper from which the text was excerpted. As it is easy to see, both checks require contact with other texts, although the traditional methodology insists on calling the first check the "reality check."

The scrutiny of the activity of reading as presented above makes it clear that reading and writing are inseparable. To read is always to write, even if sometimes without the material traces. To write is always to read, both in retrospection and in anticipation. It should thus come as no surprise that many comments concerning the reading of a text of the field equally concern writing a text from the field, and therefore most comments on writing concern an anticipated reading.

Writing the Field

An author tries to anticipate the reader's reaction in part by projecting the past criterion of the goodness of a scientific text onto the future. I say "in part" because all innovative writing hopes to establish new criteria by defying earlier ones. To be followed or to be broken, evaluation criteria seem to be helpful to a writer. A constructionist view, however, clearly reveals the impossibility of establishing such criteria a priori. As with method, there is a pattern of conventional readers' responses (known only retrospectively) and a bunch of institutionalized norms for writing that might be observed or broken in practice.

One traditional set of such norms refers to validity, the correspondence between the text and the world, and to reliability, the guarantee of repeated results with the use of the same method. These are supposedly ostensive traits: They characterize (or not) a text as it is and therefore can be demonstrated.

Validity as a correspondence criterion has attracted most criticism from recent theories of knowledge. Whether we claim to speak of a reality or a fantasy, the value of our utterances cannot be established by comparing them to their object but by comparing them to other utterances, as Goffman (1981) notes, systematically comparing various forms of talk. As the new pragmatists put it, the correspondence theory of truth is untenable because the only thing with which we can compare statements are other statements (Rorty, 1980). Words cannot be compared to worlds. A look into actual validation practices reveals that, in fact, these practices always consist of checking texts against other texts. Thus, when Ricoeur (1981) speaks of "validation of guesses," he hastens to add that by this he does not mean the application of the logic of empirical verification. "To show that an interpretation is more probable in the light of what is known is something other than showing that a conclusion is true. . . .Validation is an argumentative discipline comparable to the juridical procedures of legal interpretation" (p. 212).

One could argue that, by the same token, an observation shows that reliability can be understood as replication. From the perspective held here, however, it could be claimed that "results" are repeated not because the correct method has repeatedly been applied to the same object of study, but because institutionalized research practices tend to produce similar results. One can go even further and claim that results are as much a part of practice as methods are. An excellent illustration of this phenomenon is the recent debate within AIDS research, which shows that studies that do not arrive at what is seen as the legitimate conclusion are not funded (Horton, 1996). It is perhaps more accurate to speak of conformity rather than reliability; it is not the results that are reliable but the researchers who are conforming to dominant rules.

Dissatisfaction with positivist criteria for "good scientific texts" and a wish for alternative guidelines for their writers led to a search for a new set of criteria—within the interpretive tradition. Thus, Guba (1981) speaks of the "trustworthiness" of naturalist studies (composed of truth value, applicability, consistency, and neutrality); Fisher (1987) speaks of "narrative probability" (coherence) and "narrative fidelity" (truth value), constituting "narrative rationality"; whereas Golden-Biddle and Locke (1993) suggest authenticity, plausibility, and criticality as the ways in which ethnographic texts convince their audiences. Unfortunately, like the positivist criteria they criticize, these are again ostensive criteria of a text's success, that is, the attributes of a text that can be demonstrated and therefore applied a priori to determine a text's success.

Reader-response theory counteracts such objectivist reading theories (Iser, 1978), but in turn it tries to subjectivize the act of reading and therefore neglects the institutional effect. There is a limited repertoire of texts and responses at any given time and place, there are more legitimate and less legitimate responses, and there is fashion as a selection mechanism. The pragmatist theory of reading to which I adhere, here represented by Rorty (1992), gives preference to performative criteria. These are not rules that, when observed by a writer, will guarantee the positive reception of his or her work, but descriptions that summarize the typical justifications given when a positive reception occurs. Such descriptions do not concern the text but the responses of the readers as reported in the legitimate vocabulary of the day.

A contemporary organization theory writer who desires success might thus do well choosing postmodernism as his or her mantle, but texts written in the peak of fashion might become classical or obsolete and no properties of the text can determine which is going to be their fate. Giambattista Vico was considered odd in his time, whereas Otto Weininger is now best remembered not for his thought but for having been a success in his time.

The aspiring author cannot count on readers to know what they are going to like next, but might try to evoke accounts justifying their past judgments and hope that they will hold for a while. Two types of justifications are commonly given: the pragmatic and the aesthetic. It is even possible to claim that the latter is included in the former and vice versa, if treated broadly enough. Something "works" because it touches me, because it is beautiful, because it is a powerful metaphor, but one can also hear engineers say of machines, "Look how beautifully it works!" Rorty (1992) says that although "usefulness" is decided according to a purpose at hand, the best readings are not those that serve such purpose but those that have changed it. This he calls an *edifying* discourse or a discourse that has the power "to take us out of our old selves by the power of strangeness, to aid us in becoming new beings" (1980, p. 360). Books like Silverman's (1971) *The Theory of Organizations,* Weick's (1979) *The Social Psychology of Organizing,* or Morgan's (1986) *Images of Organization* took us out of positivist methodology, opened systems perspective, and essentialist conceptualization.

One could question the "we" of the last paragraph, claiming that this last kind of reaction is personal (many organization researchers are still using the open systems perspective) and therefore contingent on individual readers and their purpose at hand. This is a correct observation, but equally correct is to note that the purposes at hand and the ways of satisfying them tend to be limited in a given time and place. When addressed to scientific texts, objectivity—that high praise—can be seen as no more and no less than conformity to the norms of justification common in a relevant community (Rorty, 1980, p. 36)—a difficult achievement and therefore praiseworthy.

Judgments on what is objective and what is edifying are rarely unanimous (there is a variety of opinions in each community) and they change over time. Therefore, one can at best speak of a kind of writing, or rather kinds of writing, considered legitimate and read in a given time and place. The debate on what is good and bad writing can thus be usefully replaced or at least aided by a discussion of genres, that is, institutionalized forms of writing. Achieving an inventory and a description of genres not only allows for probabilistic estimates of success but also permits the understanding of deviations. Every avant-garde, vibrant fringe, every edifying discourse feeds on the mainstream, on normal science, on systematizing discourse. By the same token, the "canonical tradition" (MacIntyre, 1988) depends on deviations for its survival and owes those its eventual demise.

As long as a tradition can incorporate innovations, it is vitalized by them; the moment it cannot, it dies. This paradoxical relationship between the mainstream and the margin is well known but rarely openly recognized because it threatens the grounds of legitimacy of both the mainstream and the margin. The legitimate vision of the relationships between the two is an agonistic relationship; as in a traditional science, the best man (yes) wins.

This reasoning can be applied to itself: It is possible to imagine a nonagonistic science and an explicit awareness of the mutual dependence between the avant-garde and the retro-garde. Such views, although marginal at present, might repay in reflection and sophistication what they cost in legitimacy. It is such a view that prompted me to sketch below one possible subgenre in organization studies, the one that combines insights coming from literary theory with an anthropological frame of mind. This is *ergonography,* or a realist version of organizational ethnography (I hasten to add that my definition of realism is wide enough to incorporate not only Van Maanen's, 1988, realist tales but the confessional and impressionist tales as well).

Packaging the Field

Conventional organization field reports are written in a realist genre, often called *naive realism,* in which creating the impression of "having been there" is the source of credibility and beauty alike. Isn't realism therefore old hat, too scrubby to be put on the narrative approach I am advocating here?

The British writer and literary theorist Malcolm Bradbury, in a discussion with U.S. writer Tom Wolfe (1992), said that the reason for realism or a form of it had in his opinion never really gone away, and that "our modernist, post-modernist and therefore presumably anti-realist century" enjoys it perhaps more than ever.

This claim can be extended beyond the novel and into the social sciences, ending with organization theory. One would think that with the arrival of constructivism, relativism, and postmodernism, realism is banned once and for all. Far from it—it proliferates as perhaps never before. Within philosophy, there is the scientific realism of Rom Harré and the critical realism of Mary Hesse and Roy Bhaskar promising to reconcile constructivism and realism. Sociology is not left behind: There is the symbolic realism of Richard H. Brown, the conventional realism of Peter Manicas, the social science realism of Andrew Sayer, and the "real-ism" of David Silverman and Brian Torode. In anthropology, Bruno Latour and Clifford Geertz discuss how to achieve a realist effect without getting trapped in naive realism.

There are many demands for realism in stories about organizations; they are serious but not very specific. Stern (1973) lists three ways of understanding realism in literature and literary critique: "A way of depicting, describing the situation in a faithful, accurate, 'life-like' manner; or richly, abundantly, colorfully; or again mechanically, photographically, imitatively" (p. 40). It is against the third and in favor of the second of these interpretations of realism that the present appeal is made. A realist study does not have to denote the naive simplicity of the "it-is-true-because-I-was-there" kind of realism. Let me give some examples of works that, in my opinion, avoid such traps of naive realism.

The first type can be called *ironic realism*: Robin Leidner's (1993) study is one example, Gideon Kunda's (1992) another. Kunda's work contains a series of mininarratives illustrating life in Tech (the fictitious name of the corporation) that remain in ironic contradiction to one another. This irony is not of Kunda's making: It proves to be the way of life (and survival) at Tech. The truly skillful operators of Tech's predominant ideology shift effortlessly between the mode of total commitment and the mode of detached irony, including self-irony. Tech is a subtle culture trap, and its members live the truly postmodern life of spectators at an everlasting spectacle of which they want to be directors while performing as actors. Kunda's study reveals the paradoxical spiral of contribution and opposition to control mechanisms in which the cleverest manipulators ultimately can be unmasked as dupes and victims show how dignity can be preserved in situations of threat and anxiety. In a similar vein, Leidner shows how McDonald's, programming the manual operations of its employees to the last detail, leaves employees free to think what they please. Combined Insurance, unable to control the behavior of its agents selling insurance in the field, does not bother to prescribe operations but attempts to indoctrinate their employees' way of thinking. Instead of "solving" the paradoxes as a naive realist text would, these books preserve them, revealing paradoxicality and irony as the staple diet of organization members.

Another interesting possibility is *microrealism,* grounded in ethno-methodological approaches (an interesting sample can be found in Boden & Zimmerman, 1991). If the name were not claimed by another kind of studies, these would be called *naturalist* for their attempt to portray life in the field faithfully. My favorite work of this kind, and one that deserves to be better known, is David Silverman and Jill Jones's *Organizational Work* (1976), which describes the minutiae of job recruitment and promotion mechanisms in what appears to be a public administration agency. As through a magnifying glass we can see in the records of job interviews and similar organizational events just how an organization reproduces itself by carefully selecting and "matching" candidates according to criteria that become clear only after a conversation has taken place. Each interview contributes to the organizational life not only by producing or rejecting a new job recruit but also, and perhaps more important, by restating the identity of the organization in question. If we were to follow Van Maanen's (1988) example and look for an analogy in painting, pointillism comes to mind, so detailed is the picture.

A third possibility that comes to mind is a *polyphonic realism*: Latour's (1996) study of a project organization, *Aramis or the Love for Technology.* This is the story of a hybrid: a transportation technology project that started off by adopting the name of the handsomest of the musketeers and ended up as a piece of dead machinery in a technology museum. How did it happen? Did the machines fail, did the engineers design them wrong, did the politicians destroy the project, did competitors conspire to have it dumped? The reader gets three versions of the narrative, all realist, emitted by the voices of the field, the new sociologist of technology, and Aramis himself—all activated in a dialogue with a pupil, an engineer who wishes to learn his technoscience. This work, rich in textual devices, is especially interesting because it finds an ingenious solution to the well-known problem facing all field researchers: How to avoid smothering the variety of voices in one sleek version as well as the kind of fragmentation that occurs when all the voices are reported simultaneously.

A more modest version of the same approach can be found in my attempt to portray collective action in whole constellations of organization within the Swedish public sector. The doings in and of such an action net can be rendered by an outside observer as a multiplicity of voices coming from different sites and therefore all with their own standpoints (Czarniawska, 1997a). The simultaneous presence of contradictory narratives creates a permanent state of paradox. Resolving this paradox, the effort that Luhmann

(1991) calls *deparadoxifying,* is the daily work of those Sisyphuses of modern organizations who end their day achieving order and rationality, only to find the paradox back at their door as they come in next morning. Quasi-literary forms help render the complexity of their experience.

Such complex processes are explored in a similar vein by anthropologists (for a review, see Marcus & Fischer, 1986), ethnomethodologists (e.g., Boden, 1994), and sociologists of science and technology (e.g., Ashmore, Mulkay, & Pinch, 1989), who are also experimenting with polyphonic writings. Law (1994) and Watson (1994) employ ethnographic writing in search of illuminating not only the practices of the field but also the topic of their disciplines: social order in the case of Law and management in the case of Watson.

Ergonography, as a subgenre of organization studies, will thus have narratives as an important (although not only) material and a crucial (although not sole) device; it will additionally use the insights of literary theory as help in self-reflection. It might help to escape from the inherited image of organization theory as a defective science, which aspires to heights represented by the natural sciences without ever quite reaching them. I do not suggest that it should become a defective fiction. I argue for a conscious and reflective creation of a specific genre that recognizes its tradition without being paralyzed by it, that seeks inspiration in other genres without imitating them, and that derives confidence from the importance of its topic and from its own growing skills.

The Bright Future of the Narrative

As I was revising this text, I received the first feedback on my previous attempts to launch a narrative approach. I threw myself greedily upon them: After all, what is more exciting that to learn about what I have been doing all along? As it seems, I have been propagating a method that, when followed correctly, will place organization studies either on the top or on the bottom of social sciences (depending on the persuasion of the critic). As to a method, I cannot but quote the great narratologist himself, Roland Barthes:

Some speak greedily and urgently about method; method is all they wish to see in their work. It never seems rigorous or formal enough to them. Method becomes Law, but as this Law is deprived of any effect that would be different of the Law itself (nobody can claim to know what, in "human sciences," is a

76

"result"). Method inevitably disappoints; posing as a pure metalanguage, it partakes of the vanity of all metalanguages. Thus a work that unceasingly declares its will-to-methodology always becomes sterile in the end. Everything takes place inside the method, nothing is left to the writing. The researcher repeats that his text will be methodological, but this text never arrives. There is nothing more sure to kill research and sweep it off into the leftovers of abandoned works, nothing more sure, than method. (Barthes, 1971, p. 9)

This is perhaps not the most appropriate quote to end a book on methodology, but it expresses my deepest belief. A method is but a reflection and a convention (sometimes only the latter). Reading books on methodology does not even remotely guarantee making—and writing—a good study. Doing studies without exchanging stories with other people who did similar study, however, looks like a lonely and inefficient enterprise to me.

So, let me tell you another story. Among other things that I inflicted on my graduate students was watching a film essay by Peter Krieg (1988) called *Machine Dreams,* with the purpose of making a comparison between that work and a doctoral dissertation. We all agreed that, apart from the obvious difference—that of using moving pictures, not only words— the differences were few. Unlike novels, which we had discussed a week before, the essay contained a thesis on the genesis and development of technology, a rich field material, and quotes from scientific literature (delivered by the authors in person). It constructed a proper theory about machines—as dreams and nightmares of men. We were all fascinated by the richness and variety of material from various fields of practice: Centuries and countries whirled in front of our eyes. Who knows how much research it required.

We all agreed that it would have taken us 10 years of fieldwork alone to amass so much material. Why, we puzzled, can Peter Krieg do it and we couldn't? Somebody came up with a brilliant guess: That what Krieg learned at his film school was not the history of technology, but the skill of filmmaking. Again, no amount of courses on movie making would make everybody a successful filmmaker, but a certain amount probably would not hurt. And then we realized the paradox of the fact that, in our profession of academic teachers and researchers, we are mostly amateurs. We study the topic, not the craft. Now and then, we read books about teaching methods and research methods, books written by amateurs like ourselves.

My suggestion of the narrative approach amounts to nothing more than a systematic reflection on a craft that we are practicing while doing research. And because the core of this craft seems to be reading and writing, it seems only sensible to me to borrow both the models and the vocabulary of reflection from literature and literary theory.

What hopes should one vest in such a loan? Or, to put it in market terms, will narrative approaches deliver? And, in that case, what?

In an interesting essay titled "Narrative Dis-Curses," Betsy Cullum-Swan and Peter K. Manning (1996) take to task contemporary sociological texts that claim to be narratives—and find them wanting.

Much as I agree with Cullum-Swan and Manning's (1996) evaluations of the texts they read, I sympathize with the authors of narratives in that I see their (our) fate as doomed. This has to do with a significant difference between the social science and literary genres, a difference that I kept hidden until the end. This difference is that a part of the genre of social sciences is making explicit promises as to what a given text should achieve. Whereas the writers of fiction might, in a foreword that nobody reads, express a hope that the readers will be shocked/amused/entertained or something equally vague, the honor code of our amateurish profession requires that we ourselves forge the sword for the critics to cut our heads off.

Luckily, the consolation is in yet another look at the field of fiction. After all, there, even more than here, deadly wounds abound, although inflicted with arms forged by the critics themselves. With what results? Perhaps some authors do abandon writing and start growing roses, but most of them, it seems to me, just continue writing. It is almost as if the main force behind that insistence is that they want to say something.

Peter Krieg (1988) develops his theory of technology thus: Men constructed machines to escape their biological nature (of which women are supposedly a large part). This technical second nature brought them more disappointment than relief (after all, says Krieg, projected dreams and nightmares are only apt to return). Not all is lost, though: The disappointment with the second nature brought to the fore an unexpected gain: a better understanding of the human condition (including the role of women in the fate of humanity), something that could be called a third, or reflexive, nature.

I claim that narrative approaches are especially appropriate for exploring and expressing this reflexive nature by the virtue of being created specifically for this purpose. Those who worry that too much reflection will paralyze action—a worry common to Nicholas Luhmann and to managers—should be comforted by the claim of Umberto Eco that a critical/semiotic reader is as able as a naive reader to relate to the text directly, in addition to being able to appreciate how cleverly the text has been written.

REFERENCES

Abu-Lughod, Lila. (1991). Writing against culture. In Richard G. Fox (Ed.), *Recapturing anthropology. Working in the present* (pp. 137-162). Santa Fe, NM: School of American Research Press.

Agger, Ben. (1990). *The decline of discourse: Reading, writing and resistance in postmodern capitalism.* New York: Falmer.

Arendt, Hannah. (1969). Introduction. Walter Benjamin: 1892-1940. In Hannah Arendt (Ed.), *Illuminations.* New York: Schocken.

Ashmore, Malcolm. (1989). *The reflexive thesis. Wrighting sociology of scientific knowledge.* Chicago: University of Chicago Press.

Ashmore, Malcolm, Mulkay, Michael, & Pinch, Trevor. (1989). *Health efficiency: A sociology of health economics.* Milton Keynes, UK: Open University Press.

Astley, Graham W., & Zammuto, Raymond F. (1992). Organization science, managers, and language games. *Organization Science, 3*(4), 443-460.

Bakhtin, Michail M. (1981). Discourse in the novel. In *The dialogic imagination. Four essays* (pp. 259-422). Austin: University of Texas Press.

Bakhtin, Michail M./Medvedev, P. N. (1985). *The formal method in literary scholarship: A critical introduction to sociological poetics.* Cambridge, MA: Harvard University Press. (Original work published 1928)

Barley, Nigel. (1983). *The innocent anthropologist. Notes from a mud hut.* London: Penguin.

Barley, Nigel. (1986). *A plague of caterpillars. A return to the African bush.* London: Penguin.

Barley, Nigel. (1988). *Not a hazardous sport.* London: Penguin.

Barley, Nigel. (1989). *Native land.* London: Penguin.

Barthes, Roland. (1971). Écrivains intellectuels, professeurs. *Tel Quel, 47,* 3-18.

Barthes, Roland. (1977). Introduction to the structural analysis of narratives. In Roland Barthes, *Image-music-text* (pp. 79-124; Stephen Heath, Trans.). Glasgow: William Collins. (Original work published 1966)

Barthes, Roland. (1979). From work to text. In Josué V. Harari (Ed.), *Textual strategies* (pp. 73-82). Ithaca, NY: Methuen.

Berger, Peter, & Luckmann, Thomas. (1995). *Modernity, pluralism and the crisis of meaning.* Gütersloh: Bertelsmann Foundation.

Boden, Deirdre. (1994). *The business of talk: Organizations in action.* Cambridge, UK: Polity.

Boden, Deirdre, & Zimmerman, Don H. (Eds.). (1991). *Talk and social structure.* Cambridge, UK: Polity.

Boje, David. (1991). The story-telling organization: A study of story performance in an office-supply firm. *Administrative Science Quarterly, 36,* 106-126.

Boland, Richard J., Jr. (1989). Beyond the objectivist and the subjectivist: Learning to read accounting as text. *Accounting, Organizations and Society, 14*(5/6), 591-604.

Boland, Richard J., Jr. (1994). Identity, economy and morality in "The rise of Silas Lapham." In Barbara Czarniawska-Joerges & Pierre Guillet de Monthoux (Eds.), *Good novels, better management* (pp. 115-137). Reading, UK: Harwood Academic.

Boland, Richard J., Jr., & Tankasi, Ramkrishnan V. (1995). Perspective making and perspective taking in communities of knowing. *Organization Science, 6*(3), 350-372.

Boyle, James. (1992). A theory of law and information copyright, spleens, blackmail and insider trading. *California Law Review, 80* (6), 1416-1538.

Bradbury, Malcolm. (1992). Closer to chaos: American fiction in the 1980s. *Times Literary Supplement, 22* 17.

Brown, Colin, Guillet de Monthoux, Pierre, & McCullough, Arthur. (1976). *The access-casebook.* Stockholm: Teknisk Högskolelitteratur.

Brown, Richard H. (1977). *A poetic for sociology: Toward a logic of discovery for the human sciences.* New York: Cambridge University Press.

Brown, Richard H. (1980).The position of narrative in contemporary society. *New Literary History, 11*(3), 545-550.

Brown, Richard H. (1987). *Society as text. Essays on rhetoric, reason, and reality.* Chicago: University of Chicago Press.

Brown, Richard H. (1989). *Social science as civic discourse. Essays on the invention, legitimation, and uses of social theory.* Chicago: University of Chicago Press.

Bruner, Edward M. (1986). Ethnography as narrative. In Victor M. Turner & Edward M. Bruner (Eds.), *The anthropology of experience* (pp. 139-155). Chicago: University of Illinois Press.

Bruner, Jerome. (1986). *Actual minds, possible worlds.* Cambridge, MA: Harvard University Press.

Bruner, Jerome. (1990). *Acts of meaning.* Cambridge, MA: Harvard University Press.

Bruss, Elisabeth W. (1976). *Autobiographical acts. The changing situation of a literary genre.* Baltimore: John Hopkins University Press.

Bruyn, Severyn. (1966). *The human perspective in sociology: The methodology of participant observation.* Englewood Cliffs, NJ: Prentice Hall.

Burawoy, Michael. (1979). *Manufacturing consent.* Chicago: University of Chicago Press.

Burke, Kenneth. (1969). *A grammar of motives.* Berkeley: University of California Press. (Original work published 1945)

Burrell, Gibson, & Morgan, Gareth. (1979). *Sociological paradigms and organizational analysis.* Aldershot, UK: Gower.

Capote, Truman. (1972). Music for chameleons. In Truman Capote, *Music for chameleons* (pp. 3-11). London: Abacus.

Cappetti, Carla. (1995). *Writing Chicago: Modernism, ethnography, and the novel.* New York: Columbia University Press.

Clark, Burton R. (1972). The organizational saga in higher education. *Administrative Science Quarterly, 17,* 178-184.

Corvellec, Hervé. (1996). *Stories of achievements.* Lund: Lund University Press.

Cullum-Swan, Betsy, & Manning, Peter K. (1996). *Narrative dis-curses.* Unpublished manuscript.

Czarniawska, Barbara. (1980). Metody badan i usprawnien procesu zarzadzania organizacjami gospodarczymi [Methods for studying and improving management processes in economic organizations]. *Materialy i Studia IOZDiK, 15,* 1-28.

Czarniawska, Barbara. (1997a). *Narrating the organization: Dramas of institutional identity.* Chicago: University of Chicago Press.

Czarniawska, Barbara. (1997b). The four times told tale: Combining narrative and scientific knowledge in organization studies.*Organization, 4*(1), 51-74.

Czarniawska, Barbara. (in press). *Zmiana kadru. Zarzadzanie Warszawa w latach 90-tych* [A city reframed: Managing Warsaw in the 1990s]. Poznan: Humaniora.

Czarniawska, Barbara, & Calàs, M. (in press). Another culture: Explaining gender discrimination with "culture." *Finnish Administration Studies.*

Czarniawska-Joerges, Barbara, & Guillet de Monthoux, Pierre. (Eds.). (1994). *Good novels, better management: Reading realities in fiction.* Reading, UK: Harwood Academic.

Dalton, Melville. (1959). *Men who manage.* New York: John Wiley.

Davies, Bronwyn, & Harré, R. (1991). Positioning: The discursive production of selves. *Journal for the Theory of Social Behaviour, 20*(1), 43-63.

de Certeau, Michel. (1984). *The practice of everyday life.* Berkeley: University of California Press.

DeMott, B. (1989, May-June). Reading fiction to the bottom line. *Harvard Business Review,* pp. 128-134.

Derrida, Jacques. (1966/1978). *Writing and difference.* Chicago: Chicago University Press.

De Vault, Marjorie L. (1990). Novel readings: The social organization of interpretation. *American Journal of Sociology, 95*(4), 887-921.

d'Ormesson, J. (1971). *La gloire de l'empire.* Paris: Gallimard.

Douglas, Mary. (1986). *How institutions think.* London: Routledge & Kegan Paul.

Durkheim, Émile, & Mauss, Marcel. (1986). *Primitive classifications.* London: Cohen & West. (Original work published 1903)

Eco, Umberto. (1983). *The role of the reader. Explorations in the semiotics of texts.* London: Hutchinson. (Original work published 1979)

Eco, Umberto. (1990). *The limits of interpretation.* Bloomington: Indiana University Press.

Eco, Umberto. (1992). *Interpretation and overinterpretation.* Cambridge, UK: Cambridge University Press.

Eco, Umberto, & Sebeok, Thomas A. (1983). *Il segno dei tre: Holmes, Dupin, Peirce.* Milano: Bompianti.

Fabian, Johannes. (1983). *Time and the other. How anthropology makes its object.* New York: Columbia University Press.

Feldman, Martha. (1995). *Strategies for interpreting qualitative data.* Thousand Oaks, CA: Sage.

Fisher, Walter R. (1984). Narration as a human communication paradigm: The case of public moral argument. *Communication Monographs, 51,* 1-22.

Fisher, Walter R. (1987). *Human communication as narration: Toward a philosophy of reason, value, and action.* Columbia: University of South Carolina Press.

Forester, John. (1992). Critical ethnography: On fieldwork in a Habermasian way. In Mats Alvesson & Hugh Willmott (Eds.), *Critical management studies* (pp. 46-65). Newbury Park, CA: Sage.

Foucault, Michel. (1979). What is an author? In Josué V. Harari (Ed.), *Textual strategies: Perspectives in post-structuralist criticism* (pp. 141-160). Ithaca, NY: Methuen.

Foucault, Michel. (1980). *Power/knowledge. Selected interviews and other writings, 1972-1977.* New York: Pantheon.

Frankl, Victor. (1973). *Man's search for meaning.* New York: Simon & Schuster.

Frost, Peter J., Mitchell, V. F., & Nord, Walter S. (1978). *Organizational reality: Reports from the firing line.* Santa Monica, CA: Goodyear.

Frost, Peter J., Moore, Larry F., Louis, Meryl Reis, Lundberg, Craig C., & Martin, Joanne. (Eds.). (1985). *Organizational culture.* Beverly Hills, CA: Sage.

Frost, Peter J., Moore, Larry F., Louis, Meryl Reis, Lundberg, Craig C., & Martin, Joanne. (Eds.). (1991). *Reframing organizational culture.* Newbury Park, CA: Sage.

Frye, Northrop. (1973). The social context of literary criticism. In Elisabeth Burns & Thomas Burns (Eds.), *Sociology of literature and drama* (pp. 138-158). Harmondsworth, UK: Penguin.

Frye, Northrop. (1990). *The anatomy of criticism.* London: Penguin. (Original work published 1957)

Gabriel, Yiannis. (1995). The unmanaged organization: Stories, fantasies and subjectivity. *Organization Studies, 16*(3), 477-502.

Gagliardi, Pasquale. (Ed.). (1990). *The symbolics of corporate artifacts.* Berlin: De Gruyter.

Geertz, Clifford. (1973). *The interpretation of cultures.* New York: Basic Books.

Geertz, Clifford. (1980). Blurred genres: The refiguration of social thought. *American Scholar, 29*(2), 165-179.

Geertz, Clifford. (1988). *Works and lives: The anthropologist as author.* Stanford, CA: Stanford University Press.

Gergen, Kenneth. (1991). *The saturated self: Dilemmas of identity in contemporary life.* New York: Basic Books.

Gergen, Kenneth. (1994). *Realities and relationships. Soundings in social construction.* Cambridge, MA: Harvard University Press.

Giddens, Anthony. (1981). Agency, institution and time-space analysis. In Karen Knorr Cetina & Aaron V. Cicourel (Eds.), *Advances in social theory and methodology* (pp. 161-174). Boston: Routledge & Kegan Paul.

Gilbert, G. Nigel. (1977). Referencing as persuasion. *Social Studies of Science, 7,* 113-122.

Goffman, Erving. (1974). *Frame analysis.* Boston: Northeastern University Press.

Goffman, Erving. (1981). *Forms of talk.* Oxford: Basil Blackwell.

Golde, Peggy. (Ed.). (1986). *Women in the field. Anthropological experiences.* Berkeley: University of California Press. (Original work published 1970)

Golden-Biddle, Karin, & Locke, Karin. (1993). Appealing work: An investigation of how ethnographic texts convince. *Organization Science, 4*(4), 595-616.

Goody, Jack. (1977). *The domestication of the savage mind.* London: Cambridge University Press.

Goody, Jack. (1986). *The logic of writing and the organization of society.* Cambridge, UK: Cambridge University Press.

Goody, Jack, & Watt, Ian. (1968). The consequences of literacy. In Jack Goody (Ed.), *Literacy in traditional societies* (pp. 27-68). Cambridge, UK: Cambridge University Press.

Grayson, Lesley. (1995). *Scientific deception: An overview and guide to the literature of misconduct and fraud in scientific research.* London: The British Library.

Greimas, A. J., & Courtés, J. (1982). *Semiotics and language. An analytical dictionary.* Bloomington: Indiana University Press.

Guba, Edwin G. (1981). Criteria for assessing truthworthiness of naturalistic inquiries. *Educational Communication and Technology Journal, 29*(2), 75-91.

Helmers, Sabine, & Buhr, Regina. (1994). Corporate story-telling: The buxomly secretary, a Pyrrhic victory of the male mind. *Scandinavian Journal of Management Studies, 10*(2), 175-191.

Hennis, Wilhelm. (1996). *Max Webers Wissenschaft vom Menschen: Neue Studien zur Biographie des Werks.* Tübingen: Mohr-Siebeck.

Hernadi, Paul. (1987). Literary interpretation and the rhetoric of the human sciences. In John S. Nelson, Allan Megill, & D. N. McCloskey (Eds.), *The rhetoric of the human sciences* (pp. 263-275). Madison: University of Wisconsin Press.

Horton, Richard. (1996, May 23). Truth and heresy about AIDS. *New York Review of Books,* pp. 14-20.

Iser, Wolfgang. (1978). *The art of reading: A theory of aesthetic response.* Baltimore: Johns Hopkins University Press.

James, Willam. (1950). *The principles of psychology.* New York: Dover. (Original work published 1890)

Janowitz, Tama. (1987). *A cannibal in Manhattan.* New York: Picador.

Jaques, Elliot. (1951). *The changing culture of a factory.* London: Tavistock.

Jones, Michael O., Moore, Michael D., & Snyder, Richard C. (Eds.). (1988). *Inside organizations: Understanding the human dimension.* Newbury Park, CA: Sage.

Kaplan, Abraham. (1964). *The conduct of inquiry: Methodology for behavioral science.* New York: Chandler.

Kaplan, Norman. (1965). The norms of citation behavior: Prolegomena to the footnote. *American Documentation, 16,* 181.

Knorr Cetina, Karin. (1981). *The manufacture of knowledge.* Oxford: Pergamon.

Knorr Cetina, Karin. (1994). Primitive classification and postmodernity: Towards a sociological notion of fiction. *Theory, Culture and Society, 11,* 1-22.

Krieg, Peter. (1988). *Machine dreams.* Berlin: Barefoot Film Production.

Kuhn, Thomas. (1996). *The structure of scientific revolutions.* Chicago: University of Chicago Press. (Original work published 1962)

Kunda, Gideon. (1992). *Engineering culture: Control and commitment in a high-tech organization.* Philadelphia: Temple University Press.

Latour, Bruno. (1988). A relativistic account of Einstein's relativity. *Social Studies of Science, 18,* 3-44.

Latour, Bruno. (1992). Technology is society made durable. In John Law (Ed.), *A sociology of monsters: Essays on power, technology and domination* (pp. 103-131). London: Routledge.

Latour, Bruno. (1993). *We have never been modern.* Cambridge, MA: Harvard University Press.

Latour, Bruno. (1994). The flat-earthers of social theory. In Michael Power (Ed.), *Accounting and science. Natural inquiry and commercial reason* (pp. xi-xvii). Cambridge, UK: Cambridge University Press.

Latour, Bruno. (1996). *Aramis or the love for technology,* Cambridge, MA: Harvard University Press.

Latour, Bruno, & Woolgar, Steve. (1986). *Laboratory life : The construction of scientific facts.* Princeton, NJ: Princeton University Press. (Original work published 1989)

Law, John. (1994). *Organizing modernity.* Oxford: Blackwell

Leach, Edmund R. (1982). *Social anthropology.* Oxford: Oxford University Press.

Leach, Edmund R. (1985, November 29). Observers who are part of the system. *The Times Higher Education Supplement*, pp. 15-18.

Leidner, Robin. (1993). *Fast food, fast talk. Service work and the routinization of everyday life*. Berkeley: University of California Press.

Lejeune, Philippe. (1989). *On autobiography*. Minneapolis: University of Minnesota Press.

Lepenies, Wolf. (1988). *Between literature and science: The rise of sociology*. Cambridge, UK: Cambridge University Press.

Lincoln, Yvonne S. (1985). The substance of the emergent paradigm: Implications for researchers. In Yvonne S. Lincoln (Ed.), *Organizational theory and inquiry: The paradigm revolution* (pp. 137-157). Beverly Hills, CA: Sage.

Lodge, David. (1988). *Nice work*. London: Penguin.

Luhmann, Niklas. (1991). Sthenographie und Euryalistik. In Hans U. Gumbrecht & Karl-Ludwig Pfeiffer (Eds.), *Paradoxien, Dissonanzen, Zusammenbrüche. Situationen offener Epistemologie* (pp. 58-82). Frankfurt: Suhrkamp.

Lyotard, Jean-François. (1986). *The postmodern condition. A report on knowledge*. Manchester, UK: Manchester University Press. (Original work published 1979)

MacIntyre, Alasdair. (1988). *Whose justice? Which rationality?* Notre Dame, IN: University of Notre Dame.

MacIntyre, Alasdair. (1990). *After virtue*. London: Duckworth. (Original work published 1981)

Malinowski, Bronislaw. (1967). *A diary in the strict sense of the term*. Stanford, CA: Stanford University Press.

March, James G., & Olsen, Johan. (1989). *Rediscovering institutions. The organizational basis of politics*. New York: Free Press.

March, James G., & Simon, Herbert A. (1958). *Organizations*. New York: John Wiley.

Marcus, George E., & Fischer, Michael M. (1986). *Anthropology as cultural critique: An experimental moment in the human sciences*. Chicago: University of Chicago Press.

Martin, Joanne. (1982). Stories and scripts in organizational settings. In A. H. Hastrof & A. M. Isen (Eds.). *Cognitive social psychology* (pp. 165-194). New York: North Holland-Elsevier.

Martin, Joanne. (1990). Deconstructing organizational taboos: The suppression of gender conflict in organizations. *Organization Science, 1*(4), 339-359.

Martin, Joanne, Hatch, Mary Jo, & Sitkin, Sim B. (1983). The uniqueness paradox in organizational stories. *Administrative Science Quarterly, 28*, 438-453.

McCloskey, D. N. (1986). *The rhetoric of economics*. Madison: University of Wisconsin Press.

McCloskey, D. N. (1990). *If you're so smart: The narrative of economic expertise*. Chicago: University of Chicago Press.

Merton, Robert K. (1985). *On the shoulders of giants: A Shandean postscript*. New York and London: Harcourt Brace. (Original work published 1965)

Meyer, John, & Rowan, Brian. (1977). Institutionalized organizations: Formal structures as myth and ceremony. *American Journal of Sociology, 83*, 340-363.

Mintzberg, Henry. (1979). *The structuring of organizations*. Englewood Cliffs, NJ: Prentice Hall.

Mitroff, Ian, & Kilmann, Ralph. (1975). Stories managers tell: A new tool for organizational problem solving. *Management Review, 64*, 13-28.

Morgan, Gareth. (1986). *Images of organization*. Beverly Hills, CA: Sage.

Nader, Laura. (1974). Up the anthropologist—Perspectives gained from studying up. In Dell Hymes (Ed.), *Reinventing anthropology* (pp. 284-311). New York: Vintage.

The new encyclopedia Britannica. (1990). Chicago: University of Chicago Press.

Oakeshott, Michael. (1991). The voice of poetry in the conversation of mankind. In Michael Oakeshott, *Rationalism in politics and other essays* (pp. 488-541). Indianapolis, IN: Liberty. (Original work published 1959)

Pfeffer, Jeffrey. (1993). Barriers to the advance of organizational science: Paradigm development as a dependent variable. *Academy of Management Review, 18*(4), 599-620.

Phillips, Nelson. (1995). Telling organizational tales: On the role of narrative fiction in the study of organizations. *Organization Studies, 16*(4), 625-649.

Polkinghorne, Donald. (1987). *Narrative knowing and the human sciences.* Albany: State University of New York Press.

Pondy, Louis, Frost, Peter F., Morgan, Gareth, & Dandridge, Thomas. (Eds.). (1983). *Organizational symbolism.* Greenwich, CT: JAI.

Potter, Jonathan, & Wetherell, Margaret. (1987). *Discourse and social psychology.* Newbury Park, CA: Sage.

Prakash, Reddy G. (1991). *The Danes are like that.* Copenhagen: Greves Førlag.

Pred, Allan. (1995). *Recognizing European modernities. A montage of the present.* London: Routledge.

Putnam, Linda L., & Pacanowsky, Michael. (Eds.). (1983). *Communication in organizations: An interpretive approach.* Beverly Hills, CA: Sage.

Ravetz, Jerome R. (1971). *Scientific knowledge and its social problems.* Oxford: Clarendon.

Rice, Albert K. (1987). *Productivity and social organization: The Ahmedabad experiment.* London: Tavistock. (Original work published 1958)

Ricoeur, Paul. (1981). The model of the text: Meaningful action considered as text. In John B. Thompson (Ed. & Trans.), *Hermeneutics and the human sciences* (pp. 197-221). Cambridge, UK: Cambridge University Press.

Riessman, Catherine K. (1993). *Narrative analysis.* Newbury Park, CA: Sage.

Rombach, B. (Ed.). (1994). *Medhänvisning till andra.* Stockholm: Nerenius & Santérus.

Rorty, Richard. (1980). *Philosophy and the mirror of nature.* Oxford, UK: Basil Blackwell.

Rorty, Richard. (1982). *Consequences of pragmatism.* Minneapolis: University of Minnesota Press.

Rorty, Richard. (1991). Inquiry as recontextualization: An anti-dualist account of interpretation. In *Objectivity, relativism and truth: Philosophical papers* (Vol. 1, pp. 93-110). New York: Cambridge University Press.

Rorty, Richard. (1992). Cosmopolitanism without emancipation: A response to Lyotard. In Scott Lash & Jonathan Friedman (Eds.). *Modernity & identity* (pp. 59-72). Oxford, UK: Basil Blackwell.

Rottenburg, Richard. (1995, June 11-13). *The green card of Berlin.* Presentation at the second international conference on the public sector in common Europe, Nerano, Italy.

Sahlins, Marshall. (1994). Good-bye to "Tristes Tropes": Ethnography in the context of modern world history. In Robert Borofsky (Ed.), *Assessing cultural anthropology* (pp. 377-394). New York: McGraw-Hill.

Sanday, Peggy Reeves. (1979). The ethnographic paradigm(s). *Administrative Science Quarterly, 24*(4), 527-538.

Sandelands, Lloyd E. (1990). What is so practical about theory? Lewin revisited. *Journal for the Theory of Social Behaviour, 20*(3), 235-262.

Sandelands, Lloyd E., & Drazin, Robert. (1989). On the language of organization theory. *Organization Studies, 10*(4), 457-478.

Schrijvers, Joke. (1991). Dialectics of a dialogical ideal: Studying down, studying sideways and studying up. In Lorraine Nencel & Peter Pels (Eds.), *Constructing knowledge. Authority and critique in social science* (pp. 162-179). Newbury Park, CA: Sage.

Schütz, Alfred. (1973a). Common-sense and scientific interpretation of human action. In *Collected papers I. The problem of social reality* (pp. 3-47). The Hague: Martinus Nijhoff. (Original work published 1953)

Schütz, Alfred. (1973b). On multiple realities. *Collected papers I. The problem of social reality* (pp. 207-259). The Hague: Martinus Nijhoff.

Schwartzman, Helen B. (1993). *Ethnography in organizations.* Newbury Park, CA: Sage.

Sclavi, Marianella. (1989). *Ad una panna da terra.* Milan: Feltrinelli.

Sievers, Burkhard. (1990). Curing the monster: Some images and considerations about the dragon. In Pasquale Gagliardi (Ed.), *Symbols and artifacts: Views of the corporate landscape* (pp. 207-231). Berlin: de Gruyter.

Silverman, David. (1971). *The theory of organizations.* New York: Basic Books.

Silverman, David. (1993). *Interpreting qualitative data.* London: Sage.

Silverman, David, & Jones, Jill. (1976). *Organizational work.* London: Collier Macmillan.

Silverman, David, & Torode, Brian. (1980). *The material word: Some theories about language and their limits.* London: Routledge & Kegan Paul.

Sims, David, Gabriel, Yiannis, & Fineman, Stephen. (1993). *Organizing and organizations. An introduction.* London: Sage.

Sköldberg, K. (1992). Through a glass darkly: A critique of Sanderlands and Drazin. *Organization Studies, 13*(2), 245-259.

Sköldberg, K. (1994). Tales of change: Public administration reform and narrative mode. *Organization Science, 5*(2), 219-238.

Smith, Dorothy E. (1989). Feminist reflections on political economy. *Studies in Political Economy, 30,* 37-59.

Spradley, James P. (1979). *The ethnographic interview.* New York: Holt, Rinehart & Winston.

Stern, J. P. (1973). *On realism.* London: Routledge & Kegan Paul.

Toulmin, Stephen. (1984, December 6). The evolution of Margaret Mead. *New York Review of Books,* pp. 3-9.

Traweek, Sharon. (1992). Border crossings: Narrative strategies in science studies and among physicists in Tsukuba Science City, Japan. In Andrew Pickering (Ed.), *Science as practice and culture* (pp. 429-466). Chicago: University of Chicago Press.

Turner, Barry A. (Ed.). (1990). *Organisational symbolism.* Berlin: de Gruyter.

Turner, Victor W., & Bruner, Edward M. (Eds.). (1986). *The anthropology of experience.* Chicago: University of Illinois Press.

Van Maanen, John. (1982). Fieldwork on the beat. In John Van Maanen, James M. Dabbs, & Robert R. Faulkner (Eds.), *Varieties of qualitative research,* (pp. 103-151). Beverly Hills, CA: Sage.

Van Maanen, John. (1988). *Tales of the field.* Chicago: University of Chicago Press.

Veyne, Paul. (1988). *Did the Greeks believe in their myths?* Chicago: University of Chicago Press.

Vico, Giambattista. (1960). *The new science of Giambattista Vico.* Cornell University Press. (Original work published 1744)

Waldo, Dwight. (1968). *The novelist on organization and administration.* Berkeley, CA: Institute of Government Studies.

Warren, Roland L., Rose, Stephen M., & Bergunder, Ann F. (1974). *The structure of urban reform: Community Decision Organizations in stability and change.* Lexington, MA: Lexington Books.

Watson, Tony. (1994). *In search of management.* London: Routledge.

Wax, Rosalie. (1971). *Doing fieldwork: Warnings and advice.* Chicago: University of Chicago Press.

Weber, Max. (1964). *The theory of social and economic organization.* New York: Free Press. (Original work published 1947)

Webster's new collegiate dictionary. (1981). Springfield, MA: Merriam.

Weick, Karl E. (1979). *The social psychology of organizing.* Reading, MA: Addison-Wesley.

Weick, Karl E. (1995). *Sensemaking in organizations.* Thousand Oaks, CA: Sage.

White, Hayden. (1973). *Metahistory: The historical imagination in nineteenth-century Europe.* Baltimore: John Hopkins University Press.

Woodmansee, Martha. (1984). The genius and the copyright: Economic and legal conditions of the emergence of the "author." *Eighteenth-Century Studies, 17,* 425-441.

Wolfe, Tom. (1992, May 22). Discussion with Malcolm Bradbury. *Times Literary Supplement,* pp. 17.

ABOUT THE AUTHOR

BARBARA CZARNIAWSKA holds a chair in Management at Gothenburg Research Institute, School of Economics and Commercial Law, Gothenburg University, Sweden. Her research focuses on control processes in complex organizations, most recently in the field of big city management. In terms of methodological approach, she combines institutional theory with the narrative approach. She has published in the area of business and public administration, her most recent work being *The Three-Dimensional Organization: A Constructionist View* (1993) and *Narrating the Organizations: Dramas of Institutional Identity* (1977). She coedited *Good Novels, Better Management* (1994) and *Translating Organizational Change* (1996). Her articles have appeared in *Scandinavian Journal of Management Studies; Organization Studies; Journal of Management Studies; Accounting, Organizations and Society; Accounting, Management and Information Technologies; Management Communication; Consultation; International Studies of Management Organization*; and *Organization*.

Qualitative Research Methods

Series Editor
JOHN VAN MAANEN
Massachusetts Institute of Technology

Associate Editors:
Peter K. Manning, *Michigan State University*
& Marc L. Miller, *University of Washington*

Other volumes in this series listed on outside back cover